3-MINUTE
DEVOTIONS
FOR MEN

180 Encouraging Readings

Edited by and prayers written by Ed Strauss.

Print ISBN 978-1-68322-250-7

Published by Barbour Books, an imprint of Barbour Publishing, Inc., 1810 Barbour Drive, Uhrichsville, Ohio 44683, www.barbourbooks.com.

Our mission is to inspire the world with the life-changing message of the Bible.

Member of the
Evangelical Christian
Publishers Association

Printed in the United States of America.

3-MINUTE
DEVOTIONS
FOR MEN

180 Encouraging Readings

BARBOUR BOOKS
An Imprint of Barbour Publishing, Inc.

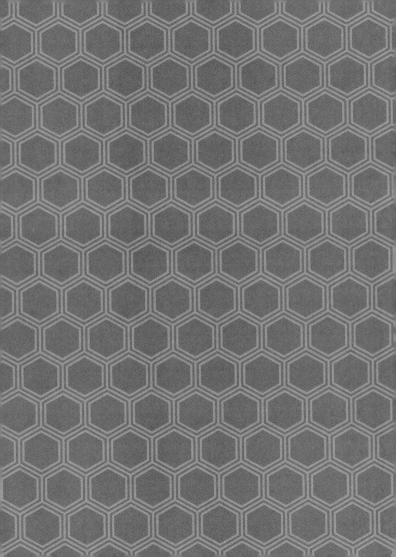

INTRODUCTION

Most days you're seeking out a moment or two of inspiration and encouragement—a fresh breath of air for the lungs and soul.

Here is a collection of moments from the true Source of all inspiration and encouragement—God's Word. Within these pages, you'll be guided through just-right-size readings that you can experience in as few as three minutes:

- Minute 1: Reflect on God's Word

- Minute 2: Read real-life application and encouragement

- Minute 3: Pray

These devotions aren't meant to be a replacement for digging deep into the scriptures or for personal, in-depth quiet time. Instead, consider them a perfect jump-start to help you form a habit of spending time with God every day. Or add them to the time you're already spending with Him. Share these moments with friends, family, coworkers, and others you come in contact with every day. They're looking for inspiration and encouragement, too.

*Your word is a lamp to guide
my feet and a light for my path.*
PSALM 119:105 NLT

DELIGHTFUL PRAYER

*Take delight in the LORD, and he will
give you the desires of your heart.*
PSALM 37:4 NIV

In this psalm, many prayers are answered, yet the word *prayer* is never mentioned. You are told to "commit," to "wait," to "delight in" the Lord, and then He will give you "the desires of your heart." But the word *pray* is nowhere to be found.

How many things do you actually "delight in"—not just enjoy, but delight in? There probably aren't many. And how many other things must you *avoid* delighting in if you are truly to delight in the Lord?

All of them. Psalm 37 treats this process of shedding all delights other than Yahweh Himself as the process of *prayer*. How do you know? Because it's the commitment to the Lord, the delighting in, the waiting for, that is answered.

Prayer is the devotion to Jesus that strengthens your reborn spirit. Prayer is the expression of desire for God to work His will. The child's eyes are on his Father. He loves what his Father loves, delights in what his Father delights in. That process is prayer.

*God, help me to delight myself in You first and foremost.
Let my heart be enraptured by Your presence. Let all my
other desires be fleeting shadows by comparison.*

LIGHT FOR YOUR PATH

The path of the righteous is like the morning sun,
shining ever brighter till the full light of day.

PROVERBS 4:18 NIV

Your way may seem unclear at times, but if you stay close to God, living in His presence, you'll share in His Spirit and His holiness. You may not feel all that enlightened or righteous much of the time, but as long as you're seeking the Lord and doing your best to obey Him, He will hear your prayers, guide you, and protect you.

Then, slowly but surely, just as the initial glow in the sky at dawn gives way to the full light of day, the sun will rise and God's blessing will be made manifest in your life. It may take awhile, and you may have to walk cautiously at first, feeling your way in semidarkness. But God has promised to be with you, so He will be.

The Bible says that Jesus, God's Son, is "the true Light which gives light to every man coming into the world" (John 1:9 NKJV). Walk in His truth and you won't be in darkness.

Dear Father, please lead me in the way I should go.
Make it clear that You're with me by giving light
to my path. In Jesus' name, I pray. Amen.

SEEING GOD IN HIS CREATION

*"But ask the animals, and they will teach you, or the birds in
the sky, and they will tell you; or speak to the earth, and it
will teach you, or let the fish in the sea inform you."*

JOB 12:7–8 NIV

Taking the time to get away and enjoy the outdoors is a pleasurable endeavor for just about anyone. But for a man of God, these activities offer something more, something of a truly spiritual nature.

One of the great things about fishing, hiking, camping, or any other activity that takes place in the outdoors is just being in the places where you can enjoy those things. These are the settings where you see God's handiwork clear of man-made distractions.

No, the creation is not God Himself, but you can learn some great truths about His nature and character by looking at the wonder of what He has created. So the next time you head out to enjoy nature, remember to think of your heavenly Father. It's in those settings where you can just enjoy His company, maybe even hear His voice, away from the world's noise.

*Father, I thank You for how You speak to me
through Your creation. Fill my heart with an awe
of Your glory, creativity, and power, I ask.*

SAVED ONLY BY GRACE

*Christ Jesus came into the world to
save sinners, of whom I am chief.*
1 TIMOTHY 1:15 NKJV

Paul wasn't just acting humble when he declared that he was the worst of sinners. He never forgot that, in his blind zeal, he had arrested and tortured numerous Christians and urged that they be killed. Looking back years later, he stated that any righteousness he once thought he'd had was "rubbish" (Philippians 3:8 NKJV).

Why did God choose such a sinner for one of His leading apostles? Paul explained that God wanted to show by *his* example that there was no person so sinful that He couldn't redeem them (1 Timothy 1:16).

However, sometimes after you've been serving the Lord for a few years, you can forget what a bad state you were once in. You can begin to think that you're quite righteous and can even start to believe that you're good enough to make it on your own. But remind yourself what Jesus saved you from, and that it was by His grace you were saved, not your own goodness (Ephesians 2:8–9).

*Lord, thank You for saving me from all my sins and
from a life full of shame and regret. Help me never forget
that it's only by Your mercy I have eternal life.*

ALL THINGS NEW

Anyone who belongs to Christ has become a new person.
The old life is gone; a new life has begun!

2 CORINTHIANS 5:17 NLT

◎ ◎ ◎

A relationship with Jesus invites you to do things you never thought you could do. Somehow, impossible reactions become possible. Jesus helps you forgive when you'd normally hold a grudge, love when it would be easier to hate, and share when you'd like to withhold. You become generous in love, grace, and gentleness toward those who enter your life. . .and not because you're expecting anything in return.

God accomplished this by entering into a covenant with you. A covenant is a contract that God has bound Himself to fulfill. God brings all the positive attributes and resources—grace, forgiveness, and love. It seems unfair. You get everything and He doesn't seem to get much, but this is the covenant God gladly accepts.

Once you have access to all God offers, you find your perceptions, attitudes, and thoughts changed. You come to Jesus just as you are, but you don't stay that way.

God, always remind me that when I accepted Christ,
I entered into a covenant with You, and You will always
uphold Your promises. Help me to rejoice in my new life.

THE JOY OF RELYING ON GOD

But I trust in your unfailing love;
my heart rejoices in your salvation.

PSALM 13:5 NIV

In light of the scripture above, begin by asking what you're trusting in or leaning on today. Are you joyful? Are you feeling fearful or frustrated? Your emotions and thoughts are helpful clues to what you think about God. They provide the evidence of a life of faith or a life attempting to get by on its own.

While following Jesus never assures you of smooth sailing, you're assured of God's presence based on His mercy for you. If you aren't joyful today and find yourself stuck in despair, it could be that you're trusting in yourself to earn God's mercy or simply relying on your own resources and wisdom to help yourself.

There is great contentment in trusting God's mercy and falling back on His help. You don't lean on God because you've earned His help or favor. Rather, you start with His mercy that assures you of His saving help and presence, whether you're going through good times or bad.

God, please encourage my heart. Help me to
experience Your peace and joy now. Draw me close
to You. I pray all this in the name of Jesus.

FAITH WHEN IT REALLY COUNTS

"Do not rebel against the LORD. And do not be afraid of the people of the land, because we will devour them. Their protection is gone, but the LORD is with us. Do not be afraid of them."

NUMBERS 14:9 NIV

Joshua and Caleb were the only two men over forty years old who were allowed to enter the Promised Land. After forty years in the wilderness, these men faced the monumental task of taking the land God had promised to the Israelites.

Their faith in God was an all-encompassing, as-if-their-lives-depended-on-it kind of faith. Why? Because their lives actually *did* depend on God's promises. If Joshua was to lead Israel into the land, he would have to feel God's presence on a moment-by-moment basis and step out in faith, trusting that God would come through for him.

Joshua's job as the leader of Israel was to encourage the people to attack fortified cities in the face of overwhelming odds. Through forty years, his confidence in God's strong arm had not wavered. And God rewarded his faith. Let Joshua's story of determined, consistent belief encourage you today.

God, please help me to have the faith and courage of Joshua, to believe that You're with me and will keep all Your promises. In Jesus' name, I pray.

CAST YOUR CARES ON GOD

Cast your cares on the LORD and he will sustain you;
he will never let the righteous be shaken.

PSALM 55:22 NIV

This passage of scripture has been a source of great comfort to millions of believers, yet some people protest, "I wish it *were* that simple! When huge problems come, do I just calmly hand them to God and He takes care of everything?" This is a valid question.

Earlier in this psalm, David spoke of threats, of conspiracies, of battles raging against him, and of the betrayal of friends. (This likely happened during the civil war when Absalom revolted.) David was able to cast his cares on God, but it wasn't a quick or easy process. At the same time, he had to lead his forces against the enemy.

And he had to pray desperately: "Evening, morning and noon I cry out in distress" (verse 17). David *continually* cast his cares upon God, until he received assurance that God would answer. Yes, you *can* simply hand small problems over to God, but when huge problems assail you, you may have to repeatedly cast your cares on Him.

Lord, it's me again. Once more, I hand my cares
over to You. Help me! I'm in a desperate situation.
I can't manage this problem on my own.

HEART PROTECTION

How can a young person stay pure? By obeying your
word. . . . I have hidden your word in my heart,
that I might not sin against you.

PSALM 119:9, 11 NLT

Gloves protect your hands. Shoes protect your feet. Safety goggles protect your eyes. What protects your heart?

Hearts are where spiritual decisions are made. The heart remains unprotected when you don't know which rules to follow. Accurate spiritual decisions can't be made when you have no idea what God has to say about important life issues.

When you argue that you have no time to read God's Word, you shouldn't be surprised when you break His law. Consuming God's Word is essential in learning how to live a godly life. Your decisions can't be made simply because you feel like it, or because the majority of people you talk to believe you should do something.

The integrity of your heart and the decisions it makes will always be based on your willingness to consult God's Word and obey it.

God, protect my heart from evil. And help me not to let
anything into my heart that would corrupt me.
Remind me to take time to soak in Your Word.

THE SOURCE OF TEMPTATION

When tempted, no one should say, "God is tempting me."
For God cannot be tempted by evil, nor does he tempt anyone;
but each person is tempted when they are dragged
away by their own evil desire and enticed.

JAMES 1:13–14 NIV

The Bible teaches that temptation comes from basically three sources: from the devil (Adam and Eve sinned when they gave in to his temptation; also, the devil tempted Jesus Himself), from the world, and from our own evil, fallen hearts.

Many young Christians come into the faith believing that they'll no longer be tempted to sin in ways they used to. Some become discouraged when they find that the temptation to sin doesn't just go away.

Temptation will always be a part of your life here on earth. It existed in the beginning for humanity, and it still exists today. But God can't and won't tempt you to sin. On the other hand, the Bible promises: "God is faithful; he will not let you be tempted beyond what you can bear. But when you are tempted, he will also provide a way out so that you can endure it" (1 Corinthians 10:13 NIV).

Dear God, strengthen me by Your Spirit, and help me to resist
temptation. In the name of Jesus, I pray. Amen.

THE HEART OF FORGIVENESS

*Bear with each other and forgive one another if any of you has
a grievance against someone. Forgive as the Lord forgave you.*
COLOSSIANS 3:13 NIV

The heart has long been the metaphor for the deepest parts of a man's emotions and thoughts. In addition to the Hebrews, the ancient Greeks credited the heart as being the seat of a person's thoughts, and therefore his actions.

Today you can extend that metaphor with what is known from science. The heart is essentially a pump for the blood, and the blood is a vehicle for oxygen to be taken to every point of the body. Without this pumping of oxygen, the body dies. The Bible therefore declares "the blood is the life" of all flesh (Deuteronomy 12:23 NIV).

Importantly, the point of a pump isn't to receive something, but to push it along. The heart wouldn't be functioning according to its design if it kept freshly oxygenated blood to itself. In the same way, if you receive forgiveness from the Lord without pushing it along, then your spiritual heart isn't functioning according to its design. A healthy Christian heart bears with the shortcomings and offenses of others.

*Lord, help me to be tenderhearted and forgiving, as You are.
You have forgiven me for so much. May I forgive
others freely as well.*

BUILDING WITH GOD

Commit your actions to the LORD,
and your plans will succeed.
PROVERBS 16:3 NLT

You may be involved in a complex project with many unsettled issues that you don't know how to resolve. Or its chances of succeeding might be slim. But have you committed the project to God? That's the way to gain peace and clarity. If you commit what you're involved in to God, He will see to it that your plans succeed.

The Bible instructs, "Commit everything you do to the LORD. Trust him, and he will help you" (Psalm 37:5 NLT). He'll help you, that is, if the project is His will. The Bible also warns, "Except the LORD build the house, they labour in vain that build it" (Psalm 127:1 KJV). Too many men try to accomplish something but haven't checked it out with God first. So their labor is potentially in vain. Whether they're building a house or whatever they're trying to accomplish, it won't succeed, or it won't last.

Before you embark on a project, lay it before God and be sure to get His blessing and authorization before you sink time and energy into it.

Heavenly Father, I submit all my plans to You.
Please have Your perfect way with them.
Help them to succeed only if they're Your will.

CULTIVATING GRATITUDE

*"Those who sacrifice thank offerings honor me,
and to the blameless I will show my salvation."*

PSALM 50:23 NIV

If there was ever a cure for being "hardened by sin's deceitfulness" (Hebrews 3:13 NIV) in a man's life, it's offering thanks to God. It's so easy to let the worries and distractions of this life pull you away from the things that matter; they make you forgetful of the blessings you've received and are living in. No action softens the heart and encourages the spirit like offering thanks to God.

The scripture often uses the word *sacrifice* in the context of thanksgiving. The first instances of sacrificing an offering to God were Cain and Abel. Abel did it well, with a genuinely thankful heart, but Cain didn't. The objects offered are not what God receives, but rather the gratitude itself.

Thanksgiving opens up the relationship God wants. Not giving thanks is a symptom of abandoning truth. Romans 1:21 (NIV) says, "For although they knew God, they neither glorified him as God nor gave thanks to him, but their thinking became futile and their foolish hearts were darkened."

*Lord, I thank You for all the good You do in my life! I thank
You for keeping me safe, providing for me, and using
me for Your kingdom! Thank You, Father!*

HOW TO CAPTURE GOD'S ATTENTION

But the eyes of the LORD are on those who fear him,
on those whose hope is in his unfailing love, to deliver
them from death and keep them alive in famine.

PSALM 33:18–19 NIV

God's attention and provision don't hinge on how well you pray. It's all too easy to think of God as a slot machine that demands certain practices in order to meet your needs. Christians often run the risk of domesticating God, demanding that He meet their needs and serve their purposes.

Those who expect provision set God apart as holy and powerful, worthy of reverence and respect. You don't pray for God's presence in order to manipulate Him for your purposes. Rather, you yield to His majestic power.

The psalmist then reminds you that God's love is unfailing. You don't fear a monstrous, angry deity; you serve a holy, all-powerful God who loves you deeply and won't fail you even if you have been unfaithful. As you rest in God's care for you, you'll find a constant, unmoving love that is deeply committed to you.

God, thank You that though You are all-powerful and infinitely
holy, You think of me. Help me to know that You are
God and that You love me and will care for me.

THERE WILL BE A FUTURE

*"I know the plans I have for you," says the L*ORD*. "They are plans
for good and not for disaster, to give you a future and a hope."*

JEREMIAH 29:11 NLT

There are no problems God cannot solve, no circumstances that
escape His attention, no future that can't be adapted to His plan.
God is never surprised, never in need of being educated, and never
in doubt. His way is perfect.

In the difficult turns of your life, you may struggle,
misunderstand, then blame God. Why? You don't know the end
of the story. You think what you face is unfair and that God not only
doesn't make sense but is untrustworthy. What He knows—but you
don't see—is that there is an ending that proves His faithfulness.
You just haven't come to that part of the story yet.

You know the beginning of your story. You're living in the
present. The future? That's the part God understands. So hold on.
Trust your loving Creator's promise that His plan is perfect and
for your good even when it doesn't seem like it.

*Lord, I love You and trust You. I know You have good things—
peace and blessings—for me. Help me to trust You through
the difficult times on the way to the future You've prepared.*

WE ALL NEED CONTINUED ENCOURAGEMENT

"Be strong and courageous, because you will lead these people to inherit the land I swore to their ancestors to give them."
JOSHUA 1:6 NIV

Joshua had seen God descend in a cloud at the Tent of Meeting, and God told him, "Be strong and courageous, for you will bring the Israelites into the land I promised them" (Deuteronomy 31:23 NIV). Since Joshua had *just* seen the Lord and heard His audible voice, why did the Lord encourage him again? Shouldn't once have been enough to encourage Joshua for the rest of his life?

No. God knew he needed further encouragement. So often you, like Peter, move forward in faith and "step out of the boat." But then the waves rise around you, and your courage wavers (Matthew 14:22–33). God knew that Joshua would be leading a fearful people into a difficult situation, and he'd need continued reassurance.

How often do you find yourself looking in fear at your circumstances rather than looking to God? You, too, need to find continued reassurance by daily searching the scriptures and by asking for the strength of God's Spirit.

Lord, my faith has faltered many times, and I have often turned to You and Your Word for courage and faith. Thank You for Your continual, unfailing encouragement.

LIVING FOR GOD

So then, each of us will give an account of ourselves to God.

ROMANS 14:12 NIV

"We must all stand before Christ to be judged. We will each receive whatever we deserve for the good or evil we have done" (2 Corinthians 5:10 NLT). There will be no hiding anything from Him in that day. "He will bring our darkest secrets to light and will reveal our private motives. Then God will give to each one whatever praise is due" (1 Corinthians 4:5 NLT).

This event is the Judgment Seat of Christ, which happens after His second coming. The purpose of this accounting is to reward believers for the good they have done. But 1 Corinthians 3:11–15 is clear that selfish works will be burned up. This ought to spur you to do your best for Christ now. You don't want to enter heaven with little or no reward.

Jesus promised that God would reward faithful, diligent service for Him and said you'd be called to give an account for idle words and an idle life (Matthew 12:36; James 4:17). It matters very much how you live.

Father in heaven, help me to live for You today
and avoid wasting time with useless deeds that
will be burned up. Help my life to count!

THE TRUE BATTLE

What causes fights and quarrels among you?
Don't they come from your desires that battle within you?

JAMES 4:1 NIV

The inner life of a man is who he really is. Proverb 23:7 (NKJV) puts it this way: "For as he thinks in his heart, so is he." The heart determines everything you do and say since it contains your value system. Solomon warned: "Above all else, guard your heart, for everything you do flows from it" (Proverbs 4:23 NIV). Scripture promises that a man's inner life will always come out:

> *"A good man brings good things out of the good*
> *stored up in his heart, and an evil man brings*
> *evil things out of the evil stored up in his heart.*
> *For the mouth speaks what the heart is full of."*
> (Luke 6:45 NIV)

When you experience conflict with others, you may be allowing the turmoil of your heart to express itself. Other people may not be "the problem." You may be engaging in the wrong battle. The real battle is saying no to your desires and wants, and humbling yourself to serve.

Dear God, help me store good things from Your Word
in my heart. Fill my heart with Your love so that what
I do and say will reflect Your presence, I pray.

SERVING GOD BY SERVING OTHERS

"The King will reply, 'Truly I tell you, whatever you did for one of the least of these brothers and sisters of mine, you did for me.'"

MATTHEW 25:40 NIV

The verse above—as well as passages like James 2:14–26—*seem* to imply that serving others is a requirement for salvation. Yet the Bible is clear that salvation is based on faith in Christ and not on your good works.

Jesus' and James's words don't contradict the message of salvation by faith in Christ alone. Instead, those who have received salvation by faith and have God's Spirit living within them will be motivated to serve out of love for God and others.

Doing good things for others doesn't make you a Christian, and it won't "earn" you salvation. On the other hand, as a follower of Jesus, you'll find yourself motivated to serve others, knowing that when you serve the "least of these," you're serving God.

Have you been wondering what God wants you to do? Ask Him first to give you the motivation to serve; then ask Him to show you ways you can serve others.

Father, I know that only You can save me. Help my life to overflow with Your love so that I will naturally reach out to help others.

WHOLEHEARTEDLY HIS

*[Amaziah] did what was right in the eyes
of the LORD, but not wholeheartedly.*

2 CHRONICLES 25:2 NIV

Religion may ask, "Are you in or are you out?" But God asks, *How far
in are you?* His interest is in an active relationship. Before the wedding,
a man is "out," but afterward, he is "in." And once he's married, the
question isn't, "Is he really married, or just a little married?

Everything God does is to have His people be "really in"—
wholeheartedly with Him. It's possible to do what is right in His eyes,
but not in a way that demonstrates a real relationship. Following the
rules is never enough for a Father. Character and heart matter more.

No one ever impressed his wife, his boss, or his commanding
officer with a halfhearted effort. The good news is that in Christ,
you are given a whole heart to be His:

> *"I will give them a heart to know me, that I am
> the LORD. They will be my people, and I will be
> their God, for they will return to me with all
> their heart."*
> (Jeremiah 24:7 NIV)

*Father, may I follow You wholeheartedly, and be tucked
under Your feathers, close to Your heart. May my life
reveal a close relationship with You.*

UNITY IN THE SPIRIT

They were all filled with the Holy Ghost. . . . And the multitude of them that believed were of one heart and of one soul.

ACTS 4:31–32 KJV

You received the Holy Spirit into your heart when you put your faith in Jesus (see Galatians 4:6). Many people are interested in what the Spirit can do for them. But they often overlook one of His chief purposes—to bring Christians into unity.

"By one Spirit we were all baptized into one body" (1 Corinthians 12:13 NKJV), so although we're individual members, we "are all one in Christ Jesus" (Galatians 3:28 NIV). We all share in "the communion of the Holy Spirit" (2 Corinthians 13:14 NKJV).

The same Holy Spirit who dwells in your heart also dwells in the hearts of other believers, and He loves each of them as much as He loves you. This is why Christians are to love one another sincerely, and why "the members should have the same care one for another" (1 Corinthians 12:25 KJV). You are to look out for them just like you would a brother or sister.

God, help me to give thought to how I can show Your love to other members of the body of Christ, honor them, and do good to them.

WHO JESUS CHRIST IS IN YOU

For it pleased the Father that in Him all the fullness should
dwell, and by Him to reconcile all things to Himself.

COLOSSIANS 1:19-20 NKJV

You probably haven't thought of even 10 percent of the questions you should be asking, let alone answering, biblically and intellectually. Still, you've probably learned and experienced much that is true— truths you can't review too often.

Do you want to know something truly transforming? Review the dozens of "who I am in Christ" statements compiled by Neil T. Anderson, and more than doubled in size by others. Untold millions have experienced spiritual healing, health, and hope by reading them.

What would happen, however, if you turned the equation around? Specifically, what would happen in your life if you began affirming what's true about "who Jesus Christ is in *me*"? When you ponder this, what immediately comes to mind? You can thank the Lord daily for His sovereignty (greatness), providence (goodness), love (graciousness), and mystery (God alone knows).

In the coming days, continue to consider the many truths about what God's Son means to *your* life.

Jesus, please reveal to me who You are—and have proven
Yourself to be—in my life. Encourage me and surprise
me with unfolding revelations of Your presence, I pray.

PRAYER THAT'S WORTH THE WAIT

When your words came, I ate them;
they were my joy and my heart's delight.
JEREMIAH 15:16 NIV

Eating is often associated with the delight of learning and meditating on the words of God. Jeremiah actively sought God's direction and relied on Him. Receiving God's words brought him joy and delight, leaving him content, as if he'd just eaten a meal.

Just as it can be hard to wait for a meal, it can also be challenging to wait on God with your prayers. Imagine someone who has patiently waited for a meal at a restaurant. When the food arrives, it's beyond his wildest expectations, and he savors each bite. Moreover, God's Word to you is life-giving for others as well. You can share what you've received with others so that they can also delight in God.

Patiently waiting on Him takes faith and trust that He will bring you the "meal" you long for. There is nothing that can restore you like the presence of God. Are you eagerly awaiting each day, leaving room for God to feed you?

Thank You for Your Word, O God. Thank You that it
gives me life. May meditating on the scriptures
bring me before Your throne today.

THE SON OF GOD IS FULLY HUMAN

For this reason he had to be made like them, fully human in every way, in order that he might become a merciful and faithful high priest in service to God.

HEBREWS 2:17 NIV

According to leading pollsters, it's quite astounding how many misconceptions people have about the Bible, about God, and specifically about Jesus Christ. Don't assume that your unsaved friends understand that Jesus is eternal—that as God's Son, He has existed for all of eternity past. There was no point at which He didn't exist.

Yet many people think Jesus was created at conception in Mary's womb. But that merely represents the point when He went from being fully God to being fully God *and human.*

It sometimes can be hard to imagine Jesus spending nine months "trapped" before birth, let alone spending years "trapped" as an infant, toddler, child, older child, young man, and full-fledged adult before starting His public ministry at age thirty. Yet Jesus Christ didn't become *barely human.* Instead, He became, is, and for all eternity will be *fully God and fully human.*

Thank You, Jesus, that though You existed as God before time began, You took on limited flesh and became a man. Thank You for doing this for my sake.

WORKING FOR A WAGE

In all labor there is profit, but idle chatter
leads only to poverty.

PROVERBS 14:23 NKJV

You may be dissatisfied with your job. This is especially true if you're beginning to experience burnout, if your tasks are monotonous, or if you're working for a boss you can't stand.

The Bible reminds you that "in all labor there is profit." You might not be in your dream job, but if it's paying work, it's better than nothing—at least until you can find something more rewarding. Paul advised Christians, "Use your hands for good hard work" (Ephesians 4:28 NLT). While you'd rather be working smart, *not* hard, working hard is scriptural.

"Our people have to learn to be diligent in their work so that all necessities are met" (Titus 3:14 MSG). You must not only apply yourself to your work, but also keep at it faithfully, day after day, month after month.

Although ultimately you'll only be fully content when you're doing what God designed you for, you can find a measure of contentment even in imperfect situations.

God, please help me! Some days my job seems like drudgery.
May Your Holy Spirit fill me and give me contentment
and joy—even here. In Jesus' name, I pray.

SPIRITUAL DEPENDENCY

*I am reminded of your sincere faith, which first lived in your
grandmother Lois and in your mother Eunice and,
I am persuaded, now lives in you also.*

2 TIMOTHY 1:5 NIV

Too often Christians let others be their compass, and when the
compass is gone, the dependent Christian has no pole to point to.
So he or she just spins. Paul wrote to Timothy, the son of his soul,
what Paul probably knew would be his last letter. In it, he gave the
key to avoiding spiritual dependency, in the passage quoted above.

There are those who feed off others' spiritual dependence
on them: some pastors, parents, or people with dominating
personalities. And then there are the spiritually dependent: they
might simply be followers or admire another's supposed spirituality.
Spiritual dependents have very little faith. They depend on others'
faith. They never grow into spiritually mature Christians themselves.

Such was not the case with Timothy. The spiritual maturity
that lived in his mother and grandmother now lived in him. If you
have a problem with spiritual dependency, start today to sink your
own roots deep down into Christ.

*God, forgive me if in any way I base my faith on other
people's relationship with You. Guide me deeper into You
and Your Word so that my faith will be rock-solid.*

A PLACE TO MEET WITH GOD

And Judas. . .also knew the place;
for Jesus often met there with His disciples.
JOHN 18:2 NKJV

⬡ ⬡ ⬡

Jesus often left Jerusalem and retreated with His disciples to the garden of Gethsemane, nestled on the slopes of the nearby Mount of Olives. Jesus chose to retire there on this particular occasion to pray in the shade of gnarled, ancient olive trees. He typically went there for prayer, reflection, and rest—away from the business of Jerusalem.

Protestants often minimize the need for a specific meeting place with God since believers can worship Him anywhere, but there's something to be said for having a designated place to meet with Jesus, whether it's your front porch, a walking trail, or your garden.

Much like having a dedicated office space helps you to focus better on your work, having a dedicated space to meet with Jesus clears away worldly distractions. Do you have a place you retire to and meet with Him? Do people in your family know not to disturb you when they see you there? If not, find that place today.

Lord, show me where You'd have me meet with You
on a regular basis. Help me to set aside time for
entering a quiet place of prayer every day.

ENTERING INTO GOD'S PRESENCE

Let us come before his presence with thanksgiving.

PSALM 95:2 KJV

In Old Testament times, the temple in Jerusalem was the place where God sometimes manifested Himself as the Shekinah glory. Thus, when people entered the temple, they went with an attitude of reverence, offering thanks to God.

Likewise today, your worship of God brings you into His presence. As a Christian, remember that you're entering into the very throne room of God. "Let us therefore come boldly unto the throne of grace, that we may obtain mercy, and find grace to help in time of need" (Hebrews 4:16 KJV). You have an audience with your Father, and He's attentive to your prayers.

But have you ever prayed and lacked faith that you were talking to God? You weren't quite sure that He was listening? The problem may have been that you failed to enter His presence *before* you began praying.

Before you begin asking God for things, make sure you've entered into His presence. And one of the best ways to do that is with a thankful heart and praise.

Dear Father, I thank You that You hear me when I pray.
I thank You for all your goodness to me, day after day.
I thank You that You're powerful enough to answer my prayers.

THE BIG DIFFERENCE

"My thoughts are nothing like your thoughts," says the LORD.
"And my ways are far beyond anything you could imagine."

ISAIAH 55:8 NLT

The biggest difference between God and you is that He's perfect, and you aren't. You let people down—God can be trusted. You ruin things—God makes things new. You tell lies—God only speaks truth. You're selfish—God gave you everything. You want your way—God knows what's best.

These differences point to a God who's incredibly wise, but He is often thought of as foolish. For instance, His Word says you lead by serving, find blessings by giving, and discover real life by losing what you thought was important. Paul even states that the cross is "foolishness" to those who don't believe, but it is "the power of God" to those who are being saved (1 Corinthians 1:18 NKJV).

Sometimes you want to try to define who God is by what you experience, but He's beyond anything you can explain. He has no beginning or end. Thankfully, you don't have to understand everything about God to admit that He's trustworthy.

Dear God, You're far beyond anything I could even begin
to comprehend. Help me to place my life in Your hands
and trust Your infinite wisdom to guide me today.

DARK NIGHT INSPIRATION

*Ascribe to the L*ORD *the glory due his name;*
*worship the L*ORD *in the splendor of his holiness.*

PSALM 29:2 NIV

What inspires you? For some, it's spending time with family. Others require the quiet glory of a scenic location. Still others' hearts are inspired by stories of people who have done amazing things. Artists get excited by beautiful subjects, while poets and songwriters are inspired by experiences and feelings.

Francis Scott Key, an American in the 1800s, was inspired. However, his inspiration didn't come from something beautiful; it came from a firsthand perspective of war. This led Key to pen the lyrics to what would become America's national anthem. The words are filled with images of battle, but they're colored with hope, because after the last shot was fired, the ragged American flag still waved in the early morning light.

You can be inspired even in your darkest times because God is with you. You may remember such times better than most, and they can become the most beautiful memories of all. What "dark nights" has He delivered you from? Have you given Him "the glory due his name"?

Father, thank You for inspiring me with hope during
even dark experiences. Help me to keep my eyes on You,
waiting for dawn to glow over the troubled horizon.

HOPE IN THE LORD

Unrelenting disappointment leaves you heartsick,
but a sudden good break can turn life around.

PROVERBS 13:12 MSG

◉ ◉ ◉

Although difficulties are woven into the very fabric of life and many are designed by God to draw you close to Him, He also knows that unrelenting problems can cause you to give up in despair. That's why He frequently sends relief.

Sometimes you can get by without the whole problem being solved immediately. But you need a glimmer of hope to know that God is with you and will eventually work things out. So you pray, "Send me a sign of your favor" (Psalm 86:17 NLT).

But how can you know that God even *desires* to do good to you? When an unknown psalmist was discouraged, he prayed, "I wait for the LORD, my soul waits, and in His word I do hope" (Psalm 130:5 NKJV).

God loves you and thinks of you, even when He seems distant. If you pray, not only will He send you a sign of His favor, but as dawn breaks after a long, dark night, He will send His cavalry charging in to rescue you.

God, I need help! Please show me You favor me!
Show me that You plan to protect me, to bless me,
and to give me relief from all my troubles.

THE LIKENESS OF GOD

But God disciplines us for our good,
in order that we may share in his holiness.
HEBREWS 12:10 NIV

Holiness is God's nature and He desires that you share it. But the concept of holiness is almost always mired with misconceptions: holiness means no more fun, holiness is a lot of work, holiness is boring, holiness means becoming "too religious."

Holiness is actually freedom. Nothing about it is restrictive when you're walking in it. And holiness is the only way for you to experience the Lord.

Make every effort to. . .be holy;
without holiness no one will see the Lord.
(Hebrews 12:14 NIV)

Of course, when you're living according to the flesh, valuing things that God says are worthless, then holiness will most certainly seem burdensome. That's because, even for believers, "the mind governed by the flesh is hostile to God" (Romans 8:7 NIV).

When you feel that holiness is becoming a burden, check your thought life, because "the mind governed by the Spirit is life and peace" (Romans 8:6 NIV). Embrace being governed by His Spirit so you may grow in His likeness.

Dear Father, You want me to be full of Your holy presence,
to be submitted to Your Spirit. So I open my life to You now, God.

BLESSING OTHERS

*"May the LORD bless you and protect you. May the LORD
smile on you and be gracious to you. May the LORD
show you his favor and give you his peace."*

NUMBERS 6:24–26 NLT

At an uncertain time in the history of Israel, when the people had
yet to settle in a land of their own, God provided a priestly blessing
for Aaron and his sons. A wandering people in search of a homeland
certainly needed the protection, favor, and peace of God when there
was so little they knew for certain. And God encouraged them to
imagine Him smiling upon them as He extended His grace to them.

As you think about the needs of others, pray that those in
danger will receive God's protection. Ask God to guide them
through uncertain times and to mercifully bless them. Pray for
God's favor and peace to be manifested in their lives.

Consider asking that God will be present for them in tangible,
peace-giving ways. As a priesthood of believers, you have inherited
the joyful role of intercession, and God has shown you how to fill
this role.

*Dear Lord, bless my family and friends, my workmates,
and the people I come in contact with daily. Show them
Your love, Your favor, and Your joy. In Jesus' name, I pray.*

PROTECTED IN GOD'S SHADOW

He who dwells in the secret place of the Most High
shall abide under the shadow of the Almighty.

PSALM 91:1 NKJV

How do you find rest when there's trouble all around you—when enemies seek your ruin and the winds of adversity are howling? You must dwell (consistently live) in God's shelter and abide (remain) under His shadow.

Much of the Negev in southern Israel is a vast, barren desert baking under the sun and blasted by high winds. Travelers take shelter behind great rocks during windstorms and rest in their shadow during the heat of the day. God is "a shelter from the wind and a refuge from the storm. . .and the shadow of a great rock in a thirsty land" (Isaiah 32:2 NIV).

Because you're a Christian, the Spirit of God's Son dwells in you. But He also said, "Abide in Me, and I in you" (John 15:4 NKJV). You must live in Jesus also. This means seeking the Lord and staying close to Him.

God is a great rock in a hostile landscape, and He is more than able to protect you. So stay in His shadow.

God, I rest in Your shadow today. Shield me and protect me,
I pray. Keep me safe, no matter what winds
of adversity are blowing.

BLAME AND FORGIVENESS

Forgive anyone who offends you.

COLOSSIANS 3:13 NLT

If you can offend God through choices you make, and if God had to send His Son to make forgiveness possible, isn't it obvious that you will sometimes offend or cause pain to others?

When you've been offended, you may believe your experience is unique and no one has ever endured the same suffering. Maybe that's true, but offenses happen to someone every minute of every day, so you must know how to respond to them.

When someone tells you, "Get over it," it sounds uncaring, as if you're supposed to say that the offense was no big deal. But true forgiveness requires *naming* the sin and who is to blame. In order for God to forgive you, He had to pinpoint your offenses. You must do the same, because forgiveness isn't trivial. You can't just say, "It's no big deal."

The only way to get over an offense is to face the issue honestly, acknowledge the hurt, and then intentionally choose to forgive specific offenses. There's more to experience in life than old hurts.

Dear God, shine light in my heart to see if I have unforgiven offenses buried there. Show them to me, and then give me the love and mercy to deal with them and forgive.

GOD'S ENDGAME

My son, do not despise the chastening of the LORD, nor detest
His correction; for whom the LORD loves He corrects,
just as a father the son in whom he delights.
PROVERBS 3:11-12 NKJV

If God sends hardship, financial problems, or health issues into your life, you may think it's because He hates you. But the opposite is true. The Lord chastens you because He *loves* you. He says, "The people I love, I call to account—prod and correct and guide so that they'll live at their best" (Revelation 3:19 MSG).

At times, you wish God would just let your sloppy behavior slide. And if He didn't care for you as much as He does, He just might do that. But He has a purpose in correcting you. He's refining you, and He invites you to join the process. Paul wrote, "Those who cleanse themselves. . .will be instruments for special purposes, made holy, useful to the Master and prepared to do any good work" (2 Timothy 2:21 NIV).

God seeks to make you into a better person, capable of great things. Are you okay with that?

God, thank You that You allow me to experience troubles.
While I don't enjoy them, I know they're proof that
You love me. So keep demonstrating that You love me.

LOST AND FOUND

*"We must celebrate with a feast, for this son of mine was dead
and has now returned to life. He was lost, but now he is found."*

LUKE 15:23–24 NLT

He ruined his father's plans. He misused resources. He lost everything. He was the day's headlines. In the muddy confines of a pigpen, he finally got what he deserved.

If you're familiar with the story of the prodigal son, you know there's more to it. At first glance it would seem the father, who had been ill-used by his son, would have had every justification to disown the boy. He could have treated the wayward youth as a hired hand—*if* he ever considered allowing him to come home at all.

His name could have been repeated with disdain by all who heard the story, but his father never allowed that. The father freed him from ridicule and shame. The father forgave the son before he even asked for forgiveness. Reconciliation began the moment the repentant son came within sight of his father.

Forgiveness offers freedom, reflects God's command to love, inspires restoration, and is the key that unlocks second chances.

*God, thank You for the many times You've received me
with open arms and forgiveness after I strayed
from You. I am truly grateful.*

KNOW IT ALL NO LONGER

*"Call to me and I will answer you and tell you great
and unsearchable things you do not know."*

JEREMIAH 33:2-3 NIV

If you aren't in a season of uncertainty, you'll soon experience one. When life begins to spin out of control, it's natural to worry about the future. You can become attached to certain outcomes and begin asking God for a particular future. Who hasn't struggled with some hard questions for God when the exact opposite happens?

When the prophet Jeremiah confronted uncertainty, the Lord assured him that he could call out and He would answer him. Of course, the Lord didn't guarantee that Jeremiah would *like* the answer he received. Jeremiah wasn't assured of clear-cut solutions.

Perhaps the answers to your prayers could take years or even a lifetime to unfold. Even the times when you think you understand God's ways, you'll find that there were layers beneath your prayers that escaped your attention. Whether or not you want to confront these mysteries, the most important thing is that this verse promises the presence of God in uncertain times.

*Lord, I don't know what's happening in my life right now.
Things aren't working out the way I expected them to.
Help me to trust You during these uncertain times.*

OVERCOMING DESPAIR

*He lifted me out of the pit of despair, out of the mud
and the mire. He set my feet on solid ground
and steadied me as I walked along.*

PSALM 40:2 NLT

The prophet Samuel had anointed David to be the king of Israel. Obviously, God planned to keep David alive so this could happen. At first, David didn't doubt it. But after living like a fugitive in the desert for several years, constantly looking over his shoulder, he found that his faith had become worn down. Finally, "David kept thinking to himself, 'Someday Saul is going to get me'" (1 Samuel 27:1 NLT).

Perhaps you're in a similar situation. You were convinced that something was God's will, so you stood strong for some time, despite severe tests. But recently you've begun to grow weary.

God encourages you: "Let us not grow weary while doing good, for in due season we shall reap if we do not lose heart" (Galatians 6:9 NKJV). The Word also says, "Fight the good fight of faith" (1 Timothy 6:12 KJV), so keep fighting and believing.

*Dear God, help me not to give up or surrender to discouragement.
Help me never to lose hope that You will protect me and have
Your perfect will in my life. In Jesus' name, I pray.*

AN OPTION WORTH TAKING

The only thing that counts is faith expressing itself through love.
GALATIANS 5:6 NIV

Let's take a look at forgiveness from the viewpoint of love. The greatest commands Jesus gave were to love God and then to love everyone else.

The greatest source of teaching about love comes from 1 Corinthians 13. Forgiveness is an essential part of love because love keeps no record of wrongs, is not easily angered, and is not self-seeking (1 Corinthians 13:5). When you can't or won't forgive, you're keeping records of the hurts others have done to you.

Does it sound as if you can obey God's command to love while refusing to forgive others? No. True love forgives. When faith is expressed through love, bitterness and resentment get an eviction notice.

Forgiveness is a personal choice that doesn't excuse sin, but it can remove the burden you carry and help to heal old wounds instead of letting them fester. And finally, forgiveness is the only chance you will ever get to restore broken relationships. So when the choice to forgive presents itself as an option, take it.

Lord, fill my heart with love so that I'll have the desire to forgive those who have wronged me. Cleanse me of bitterness and resentment. In Jesus' name, I pray.

SEEKING GOD EARLY

O God, thou art my God; early will I seek thee: my soul thirsteth
for thee. . .in a dry and thirsty land, where no water is.

PSALM 63:1 KJV

There are benefits to experiencing setbacks and problems. They
force you to draw close to God because you're aware that you can't
resolve them yourself. So you cry out to Him. That is, in fact, one
of the main reasons God *allows* you to experience difficulties.

Jesus said, "Seek ye first the kingdom of God, and his
righteousness; and all these things shall be added unto you"
(Matthew 6:33 KJV). However, many men make little time for prayer,
apart from shooting off a quick cry to God during emergencies.

Older people often have a deeper perspective on life, but you
don't need to wait till you're old to get insight. You can pray even
now, "Teach us to realize the brevity of life, so that we may grow
in wisdom" (Psalm 90:12 NLT).

This world is like a dry and thirsty land without water. The
sooner you realize that the things of earth don't truly satisfy, the
sooner you'll focus on God.

Dear God, help me to live in You whether I'm young or old.
Help me to realize that the things of this earth don't truly satisfy.

OTHERS IN FOCUS

Each of you should use whatever gift you have received to serve others, as faithful stewards of God's grace in its various forms.

1 PETER 4:10 NIV

Most people's online posts point to the best things that happen to them. They contain information that draws attention to their greatest qualities or achievements. There's nothing wrong with celebrating good things happening in our lives, but our celebration of self, especially social media's filtered, no-bad-days-ever depiction, can cause others to feel less important.

You normally take selfies and post them to show the places you've been and the people you've met. What if you were to focus on pointing out the good things happening in the lives of others? The opportunities to use social media for encouragement are greater than you often realize.

God always planned for you to invest in others. Beyond the likes and shares you might participate in online, you need to be intentional with your interactions. Don't forget to invest in other people, to reach out to your family, friends, and others whose lives may never fit into a standard shiny social media profile. Be a faithful steward of your gifts!

God, break me free from the "me-first" tendencies of modern media so that I may seek ways to encourage and inspire others.

GOD'S HEART FOR PRODIGALS

"As surely as I live, declares the Sovereign LORD, I take no pleasure in the death of the wicked, but rather that they turn from their ways and live. Turn! Turn from your evil ways!"

EZEKIEL 33:11 NIV

There's no mistaking the consequences that await those who turn away from God. But if you imagine an angry deity eager to judge you for your sins, consider this passage. Ezekiel shows a God who pleads with His people to change their ways. The Lord shows His people that there are two paths set before them and calls on them to choose obedience and life.

Each day you face opportunities to move toward God or to shut yourself off from Him. If you've closed yourself off from Him, this message applies to you as well: turn from your willful ways.

Seeing His beloved people undone by selfishness hurts the heart of God. The unraveling of our lives under the sway of sin is the last thing He wants. God is ready to forgive, to welcome you back to life. His plea for you today is simple and heartfelt: come back.

Dear God, You know the ways I've turned from You. Have mercy on me and forgive me. Please soften my heart. In Jesus' name, I pray. Amen.

OUR SECOND-GREATEST NEED

Make a clean break with all cutting, backbiting, profane talk.
Be gentle with one another, sensitive.

EPHESIANS 4:31 MSG

Your mother and father could have been all-knowing in your eyes, immune from making wrong choices—*or* they made mistakes that made you to want to nominate them for World's Worst Parents. Sometimes you can only see their mistakes long after the fact, but other times even as a kid you could have written a book on the subject of mistake-prone parenting.

Every parent makes mistakes. You might wish your parents would have been more understanding, more present, or more caring. You might wish they were more of this, less of that, or just the right amount of something.

When you become a parent yourself, you gain firsthand knowledge of the struggles your parents went through when they were trying to make the "perfect" parenting decisions. . .and then living with their mistakes. Perhaps your experience has created a new compassion in your heart for your parents.

Love is the greatest need of mankind, but forgiveness is a close second. Nobody's perfect—that's why God created forgiveness.

Father, I thank You for my parents, imperfect as they were.
I thank You for what they taught me, through both their words
and their example. Help me to forgive them for their mistakes.

KIND TO THE UNGRATEFUL

Love ye your enemies. . .and your reward shall be great,
and ye shall be the children of the Highest: for he is
kind unto the unthankful and to the evil.

LUKE 6:35 KJV

This verse disturbs many Christians. It seems so far beyond what they're willing to do that they write it off as unrealistic. But Jesus said that loving your enemies is proof that you're a child of God. Your Father loves the unthankful and is kind even to evil people, and as His child, you're to emulate Him.

You may have difficulty even showing kindness to those who don't express due thankfulness, let alone showing love to people who do evil and show no sign of repenting. Yet Jesus, after explaining God's loving nature in the verse above, added, "Be ye therefore merciful, as your Father also is merciful" (verse 36).

He doesn't expect you to be naive about where your enemies are at, but He asks you to "overcome evil with good" (Romans 12:21 KJV). He knows this is a difficult thing to ask. That's why He promises that "your reward shall be *great*" for obeying Him.

God, give me this kind of love. Help me to truly desire to be
like You, even in difficult circumstances. Help me to
have great love for others, I pray.

LOVE DRIVES OUT FEAR

There is no fear in love; but perfect love casts out fear,
because fear involves torment. But he who fears
has not been made perfect in love.

1 JOHN 4:18 NKJV

In the verses leading up to this, John wrote: "God is love, and he who abides in love abides in God, and God in him. Love has been perfected among us in this: that we may have boldness in the day of judgment" (1 John 4:16–17 NKJV).

Elsewhere, Paul wrote: "I am convinced that neither death nor life. . .nor anything else in all creation, will be able to separate us from the love of God" (Romans 8:38–39 NIV). If you're convinced that *nothing* can separate you from God's love, then you know you have nothing to fear from Him in the day of judgment.

Sometimes you may worry that you're not good enough. But none of us deserve salvation. We're all utterly dependent on the mercy of God. When you know that God loves you more than words can express, and that nothing can separate you from His love, this drives out all worry and fear.

Lord, thank You for saving me by Your amazing love!
Thank You that nothing can come between us!
Help me know these truths deep in my heart.

YOUR WILL BE DONE

He was near Jerusalem and the people thought that
the kingdom of God was going to appear at once.
LUKE 19:11 NIV

When God starts to lead, it's easy to get out ahead of Him. The *idea* of His will can become the object of your hopes. In other words, you can begin to love your expectations of God's will to the point that you stop following Him to see where His will actually takes you.

The disciples often got ahead of things, sometimes missing Jesus' will spectacularly. When Jesus was headed to Jerusalem, a Samaritan village refused to receive Him. James and John wanted to call down fire on them. But Jesus said:

> *"You do not know what manner of spirit you*
> *are of. For the Son of Man did not come to*
> *destroy men's lives but to save them."*
> (Luke 9:55–56 NKJV)

Talk about being on the wrong page! Clearly, they hadn't been paying attention to Christ and came up with a plan pretty much opposite to His. You can avoid their mind-set by staying in step with God's unfolding will for your life.

Dear God, I love Your ideas but often fail to follow You closely,
so I miss how You desire to implement them. Help me get
in tune with You and stay in tune, I pray.

ACT LIKE MEN

Watch ye, stand fast in the faith, quit you like men, be strong.
1 CORINTHIANS 16:13 KJV

In a letter to the Corinthian church, Paul tells them he plans to pass through Macedonia before visiting Corinth for the winter (1 Corinthians 16:5). In the meantime, however, he gives them several short messages.

Then he adds the admonition in verse 13 you see above. They are to stand fast in the faith and to "quit like men." At the time the King James Version was translated, this phrase didn't mean "to give up." It meant the *opposite*! It meant "act like men." In other words, Paul was telling them to stand fast and not give up.

Here's how Matthew Henry describes this phrase in his *Commentary on the Whole Bible*: "Act the manly, firm, and resolved part: behave strenuously, in opposition to the bad men who would divide and corrupt you. . .show yourselves men in Christ, by your steadiness, by your sound judgment and firm resolution."

Consider worldly men around you. Are they seeking to corrupt you? Stand firm against them, determined to stay true to the faith.

Father in heaven, breathe resolve and courage into my spirit so that I'll be strong in my convictions. Help me to take a stand for the truth and not retreat.

SERVICE WITH A SMILE

Whatever your hand finds to do, do it with your might.

ECCLESIASTES 9:10 NKJV

The business world has appropriated many Christian principles in slogans such as "We go the extra mile." Jesus was the one who said, "Whoever compels you to go one mile, go with him two" (Matthew 5:41 NKJV), yet it sometimes seems like commerce has grasped the value of this principle better than Christians.

In Paul's day, there were many slaves in the Roman Empire, and he gave them the following advice:

> *Obey your earthly masters in everything; and
> do it, not only when their eye is on you and to
> curry their favor.... Whatever you do, work at
> it with all your heart, as working for the Lord,
> not for human masters.*
> (Colossians 3:22–23 NIV)

You may work for a business that prides itself on "service with a smile." The message they want you to send to your customers is that this isn't just a sale, but you genuinely care about them. These are Christian principles, so you should practice them not only while on the job, but also in your personal life.

*God, please help me to be wholehearted, caring,
and cheerful on the job, delivering excellent service.
And help me to be that way in my personal life as well.*

THE WEAK GAIN STRENGTH

[God said,] My strength comes into its own in your weakness.

2 CORINTHIANS 12:9 MSG

There was a time when people gathered on Saturday afternoons at their local theater and purchased tickets to watch the latest western. Every cowboy had a firearm and was gifted in the art of being self-sufficient. These self-made men pulled themselves up by the bootstraps, and while they offered help to others, they didn't seem to need any help themselves.

Moviegoers mistakenly believed that the Bible said, "God helps those who help themselves." Men didn't want to bother God and thought they were doing Him a favor by keeping their problems to themselves. Others would simply deny their struggle and hope that their luck would take a turn for the better.

The Bible has never suggested you go it alone. The closest theme might be that God helps those who *ask for help.* Why would you need a Savior if you could save yourself? Why would you want a Savior who wasn't strong enough to handle your struggles? Let His strength make up for your weakness.

Lord, thank You for the many things I'm able to do.
You've given me many gifts. I also thank You for my areas
of weakness and inability that remind me I need You.

THANKLESS FAITHFULNESS?

For it seems to me that God has put us apostles on display at the
end of the procession, like those condemned to die in the arena.
We have been made a spectacle to the whole universe.

1 Corinthians 4:9 niv

What is the sign of God's blessing on a Christian leader? As Paul sought to correct the perceptions of the Corinthian church, he called on the image of prisoners being led to die in the arena at the hands of gladiators and wild animals.

Paul argued that the apostles who founded the church were not talented speakers or respectable individuals you'd put on display. Rather, the people doing the essential work of ministry were the ones who got tossed into the arena for sport and entertainment.

However, there's an encouraging aspect to his message: you need not be a wise teacher, an experienced orator, or a flashy miracle worker in order to share the Gospel message. God uses plain, simple people who commit to doing the hard work of ministry day in and day out. They aren't recognized and they don't stand out.

God, so much of living for You seems like a thankless job.
Things very often don't turn out the way I expect.
But help me keep my eyes on the heavenly reward.

EVERY DAY A BATTLEFIELD

So I say, walk by the Spirit, and you will not gratify the desires of the flesh. For the flesh desires what is contrary to the Spirit, and the Spirit what is contrary to the flesh.

GALATIANS 5:16–17 NIV

For the follower of Christ, there is no day without a battle. Some days it rages harder than others, but there's never a truce between the Spirit and the flesh. They're opposed to each other. One is life and peace, the other death (Romans 8:6).

You're born into this conflict when you become God's child. So how do you prepare yourself for it? The Galatians had fallen back into keeping the law, which never did have the power to win that battle. The flesh was always stronger than rules and regulations. The only thing that wins against desire is a stronger desire.

To avoid siding with the flesh, you must cultivate a *stronger* desire to walk with the Spirit. Walking by the Spirit means you're growing a greater desire for the things of the Spirit every day.

Lord, help me to yield to Your Holy Spirit, to walk in Your love and seek to please You. Help me to overcome my sinful nature by Your power. In Jesus' name, I pray.

THANKS FOR THE MEMORIES

Some trust in chariots, and some in horses;
but we will remember the name of the Lord our God.

PSALM 20:7 NKJV

Her name was Betty Jo, and she loved to visit nursing homes. By her own admission, she couldn't sing, but she tried. In her broken voice, Betty Jo seemed to perform miracles. She sang hymns, and men and women who'd withdrawn to a place of internal refuge brightened.

Her songs caused them to "remember the name of the Lord [their] God." Light came to their eyes and their lips began to move. Soon their voices could be heard, and when the singing was over, many enjoyed a visit with her.

When you're overwhelmed and suffer from a lack of inspiration, when you're tempted to trust in your strength or money or hard work (modern "chariots" and "horses"), it's remembering God's faithfulness that changes your heart. Proverbs tells you, "The name of the Lord is a fortified tower; the righteous run to it and are safe" (Proverbs 18:10 NIV).

You honor God best when you remember His goodness and let that inspire you—today, tomorrow, and into eternity.

Lord, stir my memory and rekindle my fire for You.
Help me remember Your name and all the marvelous
things You've done for me in years past.

FAITHFUL, BLESSED WORKERS

He that is faithful in that which is least is faithful also in much.
LUKE 16:10 KJV

Joseph was taken as a slave to Egypt, and he could have bemoaned his fate. But Joseph's work ethic came to the fore:

> Potiphar. . .realized that the LORD was with
> Joseph, giving him success in everything he
> did. . . . So he soon made Joseph his personal
> attendant. He put him in charge of his entire
> household and everything he owned.
> (Genesis 39:3–4 NLT)

Joseph was soon promoted to be Potiphar's assistant. Finally, when Potiphar realized *how* capable Joseph was, he gave him "complete administrative responsibility" over his estate.

Jesus told a parable about a wealthy man who rewarded two servants and told them both, "You have been faithful with a few things; I will put you in charge of many things" (Matthew 25:21 NIV). Be diligent in the details, and God will bless you.

God isn't the only one who rewards diligent, hard work. When your overseers realize that you have a superior work attitude, they'll advance you as well.

Lord, help me to be diligent and faithful at my job, not only when I'm seeking a promotion, but even when I think no one is watching.

KEEPING THE FAITH

*For we have spent enough of our past lifetime in doing the will
of the Gentiles—when we walked in lewdness, lusts, drunkenness,
revelries, drinking parties, and abominable idolatries.*

1 PETER 4:3 NKJV

The Jews living among the pagan Greeks had picked up many
of their bad habits: lewdness, lust, drunkenness, revelry, partying,
and idolatry. After they became Christians, however, Peter called
them to live differently than the world.

A few years ago, a George Barna poll revealed that "61 percent
of today's twenty-somethings who had been churched. . .during
their teen years are now spiritually disengaged"—meaning they
don't attend worship, read their Bibles, or pray. But young people
aren't the only ones who are walking away from their faith. Many
older adults are also.

First Timothy 4:1 warns that in the last times many will depart
from the faith. But it doesn't have to happen in your family. You've
probably spent enough of your past life following the desires of the
flesh, so if you're married, teach your family to avoid these pitfalls.
If you're unmarried, gather with other believers and encourage
one another.

*God, help me to be zealous in my love for You. And lead me
to speak to those who are faltering and growing weary.
May I encourage them today.*

LOVE THAT ENDURES IN TRIALS

"You loved Me before the foundation of the world."

JOHN 17:24 NKJV

You may have thought that the fact that God loves you would ensure you'd be spared most trials and suffering. So when troubles came your way, you may have concluded that you'd messed up. Jesus' prayer before His suffering should jolt you out of such notions.

Jesus was certain that God loved Him, and had loved Him for an eternity before Creation. So even though Jesus faced a violent and painful death, He didn't doubt His Father's love for Him. At the start of Jesus' ministry, the Father assured Him—and those present—of His love for His Son. In His darkest trials, Jesus returned to this. Even if God didn't spare Him from the cross, Jesus held fast what He knew of His Father.

Never doubt in the darkness what God has shown you in the light. So much of spiritual perseverance depends on your remembering how God has acted for you in the past. Trust that the God who was present then will be there for you in the future.

Dear Father, You loved me before I ever came to You,
and proved Your love by sending Jesus to die in my place.
Help me never to doubt these things.

GOD CARES ENOUGH TO ACT

Anyone who wants to approach God must believe both that he exists and that he cares enough to respond to those who seek him.

HEBREWS 11:6 MSG

You can believe in God yet lack faith that He cares enough to respond to your heartfelt prayers. Many men have been disappointed when past prayers weren't answered and have come to believe that God doesn't usually involve Himself with people today.

They basically believe that God has already done as much as He is ever going to do, and that from here on, it's up to people to work hard, seize opportunities, and take care of themselves. Small wonder that they don't bother to spend time in prayer! They think they can manage life without God's help.

Now, God expects you to work hard to provide for your needs, and He expects you to think hard to solve problems, but He's still active in the world. He still helps the helpless. Yes, He cares. And yes, He responds to those who earnestly seek Him. But you have to continually seek Him and not give up.

God, help me to believe not only that You're there, but that You're there for me. Help me to diligently seek You and not give up when You don't answer immediately.

THAT'S VERY GOOD

Then God looked over all he had made,
and he saw that it was very good!
GENESIS 1:31 NLT

Pharmaceutical companies spend millions of dollars to develop new drugs that may include unpleasant side effects. God spoke, the world came into being—and it was *good.* Thomas Edison spent years trying to figure out the right way to make a lightbulb, but God simply said, "Let there be light," and there was light—and it was *good.*

A factory worker blends chemicals and colors to produce a fake flower. God made living flowers of all different colors, sizes, and scents. The Bible says they're more beautiful than the clothing kings wear. No wonder God scattered them over the entire earth.

Anything you've made, God has made better. His extravagant imagination created birds, fish, and animals of every description, mountains of every size, rivers and lakes, and a rich palette of humanity. And if that wasn't extravagant enough, God formed the stars, named them, and flung them into space.

It shouldn't surprise you that you enjoy creating new things. After all, you were made in the image of God, and He *creates.*

God, I marvel at Your creativity in nature—from the astronomical
wonders to the microscopic marvels that scientists continue
to discover day after day. You're awesome, God!

TRUE AND REASONABLE FAITH

*Always be prepared to give an answer to everyone who
asks you to give the reason for the hope that you have.*

1 PETER 3:15 NIV

Many Christian men know little about their faith. If asked to give
reasons why they believe in Jesus, they don't know what to answer.
They really haven't given much thought to it.

However, the same person may give *very* careful thought to his
business plans. After all, a great deal of money is riding on them
being right. Yet much *more* is riding on whether his faith is true
or not. And Christianity can stand up to close scrutiny.

When a Roman governor protested that Paul was out of his
mind for believing in Jesus, Paul replied, "I am not insane....What
I am saying is true and reasonable" (Acts 26:25 NIV). The Christian
faith not only is true, but also makes sense.

If you're too busy to study the matter yourself, avail yourself
of the resources that are available—books by writers like Josh
McDowell and Lee Strobel. Investigate your faith. Then you can
be a more effective witness for Jesus.

*God, help me learn about the foundations of my faith.
And help me know how to explain what I believe
to others. In Jesus' name, I ask.*

NO MORE PRETENSE

. . .no more lies, no more pretense. Tell your neighbor the truth.
In Christ's body we're all connected to each other, after all.
When you lie to others, you end up lying to yourself.

EPHESIANS 4:25 MSG

You may say you're doing fine when you should ask for prayer. Or you may nod your head in agreement during a sermon, even though you don't fully agree. You may pray in the company of others, even if your private prayer life is almost nonexistent.

In the verse above, Paul is calling for an end to pretense. He isn't necessarily saying you should wear your heart on your sleeve, or that you should disagree out loud in church. But he *is* saying that pretense comes with a cost. When you mislead one another, you not only harm the body but end up misleading yourself.

Consider the church you attend. Do you ever see pretense in others? How does this affect your relationship with them? If you can see pretense in *others*, they can probably see it in *you*. Resolve to tell the truth, knowing that it will make for healthier, more authentic relationships.

Dear God, help me not to hide spiritual apathy under a
Christian facade. Help me to be honest. Not disagreeable
and unpleasant, but honest.

THE ONLY WAY TO DEFEAT SIN

So I say, let the Holy Spirit guide your lives. Then you won't
be doing what your sinful nature craves.
GALATIANS 5:16 NLT

Discipline, intentional action, and accountability are all good things that can help you overcome your sinful desires. You can't live as a faithful disciple by accident. However, the only way you'll consistently overcome sin is by yielding to the Holy Spirit. Then you'll begin to recognize the power of your carnal desires and your inability to overcome them.

The "self" will not fade away if you deny it. Your cravings are too powerful, and you can only educate yourself so much about the consequences of sin. At a certain point, you need a guide to redirect your desires toward the presence and power of God.

Ironically, the only way to overcome sin is to stop fighting it. You won't be shaped into a man of God by what you deny but rather by whom you yield to. By yielding your will to God, you'll have a new craving for His presence and discover that you're becoming a renewed person.

Lord, help me to quit trying so hard in my own strength.
Help me instead to yield to You. Give me a deep
love for You and a desire to obey You.

BURNING WITH HOLY FIRE

They asked each other, "Were not our hearts burning
within us while he talked with us on the road
and opened the Scriptures to us?"

LUKE 24:32 NIV

On the day of Jesus' resurrection, two of His followers left Jerusalem for the nearby town of Emmaus. They'd been overwhelmed by Jesus' death a few days earlier, and disturbed by some women who reported that His body had disappeared from the tomb. Then the resurrected Christ joined them on their journey, though "they were kept from recognizing him" (Luke 24:16 NIV).

They poured out their disappointment to Jesus, who gently rebuked their lack of faith (Luke 24:25) and then opened the scriptures to them.

> *And beginning with Moses and all the*
> *Prophets, he explained to them what was said*
> *in all the Scriptures concerning himself.*
> (Luke 24:27 NIV)

Imagine having the Author of the sacred writings explain everything about His Word to you. But even then, it wasn't until Christ revealed Himself that their eyes were spiritually opened (Luke 24:30–31). Today you walk the road to Emmaus whenever you rely on the Holy Spirit to reveal more to you (John 14:26).

God, I thank You for the times I've fellowshipped deeply
with You, and You opened up Your Word to me.

RELATIONSHIPS BEFORE CAREERS

*"What kind of deal is it to get everything you want but lose
yourself? What could you ever trade your soul for?"*
MATTHEW 16:26 MSG

● ● ●

One of the easiest responsibilities a man can take on is the financial
care of his family. Easy? Yes. Because men are prone to become
workaholics. When you're told to provide for your family, you
tackle that by focusing your time, talent, and energy to turn your
work ethic into cash.

David, Samuel, and Eli were godly men who struggled with
giving attention to their kids because work always came before
being a dad. Making money is often the easy part. Being a dad
is much harder because it requires an emotional investment. It's
easier to earn a living than to be a parent. It's easier to work than
to listen to your kids' struggles.

Because God is your Father, you can learn from Him. He's
always accessible, listening, and understanding your struggles
enough to offer perfect advice.

Never sacrifice your family on the altar of personal achievement.
It may be possible to have wealth *and* a close family, but real
relationships need to come before all else.

*Dear Father in heaven, help me not to neglect taking time to
bond with my children, nurture them, show them attention,
correct them, and laugh with them.*

FIGHT LIKE MEN

Keep your eyes open, hold tight to your convictions, give it all you've got, be resolute, and love without stopping.
1 CORINTHIANS 16:13-14 MSG

Are you facing a belligerent enemy in some area of your life? Is one of your children going through a crisis that demands your time? Are financial problems putting you at risk of losing your home? These and many other challenges show what you're made of.

When Nehemiah and his men were surrounded by enemies, he encouraged them, saying, "Remember the Lord, who is great and glorious, and fight for your brothers, your sons, your daughters, your wives, and your homes!" (Nehemiah 4:14 NLT).

Sometimes problems go on and on and become serious threats. Then they can seem so overwhelming that you feel like throwing up your hands in despair. But that's when you need to be resolute. Have courage and don't give up.

Certain things are worth fighting for and giving all you've got. That's how you win battles and withstand the onslaughts of the enemy.

Lord, help me to stand strong and give it my all!
Help me to be resolute and not give in to despair. Give me the conviction that these things are worth fighting for.

THE RIGHT CANDIDATE

Pride lands you flat on your face;
humility prepares you for honors.
PROVERBS 29:23 MSG

If you spend time in God's Word, you'll notice that the men God used never seemed quite ready for the job they were asked to do. They were fearful, impulsive misfits, oddballs, and sinners, often the least ideal candidates to do something for God. These men were entirely average, ordinary, and perhaps the last to be picked for a team.

Do you ever feel average or below average? Then you might be the right candidate God can use to do something incredible. God never wanted men who *knew* they could do something big. He likes using men who know they need *His* help.

God may set aside those who believe that He's fortunate to have them as part of His team. God sees pride as a barrier to usefulness.

So when you feel a little inadequate, out of your element, or lacking in the skills God might need, you shouldn't be surprised when God gives you something only you can do—with His help.

God, I feel so inadequate for a job I'm called to do.
Help me and encourage me in this. And forgive me for
the times I thought I was Your gift to the world.

THE TEAM

You use steel to sharpen steel, and one friend sharpens another.
PROVERBS 27:17 MSG

Everything in life has a purpose, and every purpose needs a team. For instance, if you're playing baseball, you'll need eyes to see the ball, arms to swing the bat, legs to run the bases, and muscles to do everything with precision—and that's only part of the team. You haven't even talked about head and shoulders, knees and toes.

The team Jesus had in the last three years of His life were called *disciples*. This twelve-man team worked together, ate together, and learned together. They would become the core of the first-century church.

As a Christian man, you need the encouragement of other Christian men. This can come through Bible study, accountability partners, and acts of service to others. You each have a place in the body of Christ. You each have a job that you were created to complete. You each need to recognize the contributions of others. Be sure to sharpen those around you and allow yourself to be sharpened so you can be the most effective team for Christ.

God, help me work together well with those who are on my team.
Help me to do my part, however humble or insignificant.
And may I be an encouragement to others.

WHO GETS THE CREDIT?

Deliver me, my God, from the hand of the wicked, from the
grasp of those who are evil and cruel. For you have been
my hope, Sovereign Lord, my confidence since my youth.
From birth I have relied on you. . . . I will ever praise you.

PSALM 71:4–6 NIV

The psalmist said that his praise would always be of the Lord, who was his strength. Who usually gets the credit in your life? It's easy to get wrapped up in your own plans, talents, and worries, but are you trusting God to guide you? Are you depending on Him to provide your needs, to empower you to serve others, and to help you accomplish your work?

The above scripture shows that God is able to support you and strengthen you. You don't have to rely on your own discipline, willpower, or plans. When trouble comes, you can cry out to God for help. Even if you've been distant or depended on yourself, you can return to Him. God wants you to depend on Him and won't leave you if you put your hand in His.

Lord, I cry out to You! Help me today. Give me strength
and wisdom. Guide me. I pray all this in the
name of Your Son, Jesus. Amen.

SHARPENING SUCCESS

If the ax is dull, and one does not sharpen the edge,
then he must use more strength; but wisdom brings success.

ECCLESIASTES 10:10 NKJV

If you've ever tried to cut down a tree with an ax instead of a chainsaw, you know how much work it can be. And if you've ever tried to do it with a *dull* ax, you know it's almost impossible. If you don't sharpen the ax beforehand, you'll wear yourself out.

What does this proverb have to say to you? How have you exhausted yourself by exerting more and more effort for very little return?

Does your work leave you worn out? Do you need more education or training to see results? In relationships, are you constantly frustrated? Does sharpening the ax mean becoming a better listener? Being more patient? What does success look like in your personal life? What goals have you had for years with no real results? Getting on a budget? Sharing your faith?

The challenge of this proverb is to identify where you're exhausting yourself and take the time to seek God's wisdom. He gives wisdom to all those who ask (James 1:5).

Father, give me the wisdom of Your Spirit today, I pray!
Give me a clear understanding of where I'm at
so I can seek ways to improve.

WHAT WILL YOU CELEBRATE?

This is the day the LORD has made.
We will rejoice and be glad in it.
PSALM 118:24 NLT

If you could personally create any holiday, what would you celebrate? If you wanted to rejoice in your children's good grades, then this would be a good day. The same is true for remembering the first time you read through the entire Bible, proposed to your wife, tried cauliflower, or overcame a bad habit.

You could use the day to celebrate something good that has happened to someone you know. Maybe you could let your kids decide what they'd celebrate. (You're bound to learn something.) Choose both meaningful and goofy reasons for celebration.

Maybe it would just be enough to revel in this day the same way you can every other day. God made it and that's the best reason to cheer.

It might even be meaningful to wait until the day is over and name this day for the specific ways you saw God work in your family. There's no wrong way to do it as long as you're full of gratitude and praise for what He has done!

God, thank You for this day. May I enjoy it and find reasons
to praise You when it ends. Help me to worship You,
to be productive, and to be grateful.

GAINING WEALTH GOD'S WAY

*Dishonest money dwindles away, but whoever gathers
money little by little makes it grow.*

PROVERBS 13:11 NIV

According to many people, the way to get ahead is to make false claims on your income tax, to overcharge for goods or services, and to cut corners on quality. But people find out if you're dishonest, and your business will suffer.

God's way to financial prosperity is to gather money honestly little by little and diligently set it aside in a savings account. If you start early enough, you'll eventually earn compound interest. There are no shortcuts, no maps leading to pirate treasure, and no leprechauns guiding you to a pot of gold.

Solomon pointed out the best way to build your retirement savings: "Take a lesson from the ants. . . . Learn from their ways and become wise! Though they have no. . .ruler to make them work, they labor hard all summer, gathering food for the winter" (Proverbs 6:6–8 NLT). Being faithful day after day is the best way to build a successful life, career, and savings account.

*Dear God, help me to find ways to set aside money,
even though at times it seems like I have nothing to put into
savings. Supply the money, please, and help me handle it wisely.*

STANDING IN THE GAP

"I sought for a man among them who would make a wall, and stand in the gap before Me on behalf of the land, that I should not destroy it."

 EZEKIEL 22:30 NKJV

When God commissioned Ezekiel to chronicle the sins of Jerusalem, Ezekiel listed murdering, having idols, dishonoring parents, oppressing strangers, mistreating orphans and widows, bribing, extorting, and violating God's law. Jerusalem had become a den of iniquity.

Sin causes gaping breaches in a people's spiritual defenses, and the enemy of their souls can then enter and destroy that nation. So God looks for a man who will stand in the gap, in prayer, to prevent it from being destroyed. Sadly, in this case He found no one. The people were caught up in sin, and no godly men were praying for them.

Nations fall as people become trapped in bad habits. Falling away can be so subtle you don't recognize it's happening. A compromise here and there, and before you know it, you've lost your city. God is looking for men to stand in the gap to intercede for their nation. Will you?

Lord, Samuel said it'd be a sin if he stopped praying for his people (1 Samuel 12:23). Help me to pray fervently and faithfully for my land. Have mercy, O God!

TRUST HIM MORE

*When I get really afraid I come to you in trust. I'm proud to praise
God; fearless now, I trust in God. What can mere mortals do?*

PSALM 56:3-4 MSG

We survive in a world of broken promises. You may respond to this
by putting up walls, keeping things to yourself, and never really
believing anyone who says, "Trust me."

God encourages you to trust Him. He supplies the air you
breathe and the sunshine you enjoy. In fact, He holds everything
in His creation together (Colossians 1:17), even your very self—"For
in him we live and move and have our being" (Acts 17:28 NIV).

You may still hesitate and say, "I'm not sure I can trust Him."
God is someone more and different than humans. And He always
keeps His promises (Numbers 23:19). The more you trust God, the
more trustworthy you find Him. The more you trust His love, the
less fearful you become. The more you trust in the Lord, the less
ominous life appears.

When it's hard to trust others, it's the perfect time to trust God.

*Dear Father, I usually can't see You at work, but I know You
care for me, protect me, and provide my needs.
Help me to trust You more, I pray.*

KEEP HIS COMMANDMENTS

"If you love Me, keep My commandments."

JOHN 14:15 NKJV

Do you wonder at times whether your faith is genuine, whether you truly *know* God? Many Christians ask themselves this. The Bible even advises, "Examine yourselves as to whether you are in the faith. Test yourselves" (2 Corinthians 13:5 NKJV).

And *how* do you test yourself? The apostle John gave a very simple litmus test. He wrote, "By this we know that we know Him, if we keep His commandments" (1 John 2:3 NKJV).

But which commandments are most important? According to Matthew 22:36–39, the two greatest commands are to love God with all your heart and to love others as you love yourself. John also said, "This is His commandment: that we should believe on the name of His Son Jesus Christ and love one another" (1 John 3:23 NKJV).

It's absolutely foundational to love God and His Son, and to genuinely love your neighbor. If you have this foundation in place, you can be assured that your faith is genuine, and you'll also be certain to grow as a Christian.

God, help me to love You with all my heart and to sincerely love others. Help me to be so close to You that I won't doubt that You've saved me. In Jesus' name, I pray.

SEEING YOURSELF RIGHTLY

For he knows how we are formed,
he remembers that we are dust.

PSALM 103:14 NIV

As your Creator, God knows you were made from the dust of the earth (Genesis 2:7). He knows you are a "jar of clay" (2 Corinthians 4:7 NIV), a mere "mist that appears for a little while and then vanishes" (James 4:14 NIV). God knows your power is limited. . . even if you forget.

And you regularly forget. It's easy to think too highly of yourself and depend on your own strength in a way that dust wasn't designed for. Pride may tell you you're invincible and powerful, but God knows the truth. Thankfully, He's moved with compassion when He sees your vulnerability (Psalm 103:13–14). And as a good Father, He patiently disciplines you (Hebrews 12:9).

While you may spend your time making great plans, God spends His time making great sons. He will always choose your character over your success. Ask Him to open your eyes to your own limitations, allowing them to keep you leaning on Him.

God, I'm painfully aware of my limitations. I ask You to keep
me from being proud about my accomplishments.
May I lean on You and count on You to
do the miracles I need.

NEXT QUESTION

"Don't bargain with God. Be direct. Ask for what you need.
This isn't a cat-and-mouse, hide-and-seek game we're in."
MATTHEW 7:7 MSG

It's easy to think that God can ask questions and you can't. However, the Bible is filled with questions, and most come from people who just wanted to understand God a little better.

Some questions had obvious answers, while others were more difficult. Some questions came from a place of great pain, while others were used to clarify. Some questions were spoken to try to trap Jesus, while He asked questions that made His hearers think.

It's natural to have questions, normal to want to learn, and nice to get an answer. God isn't frustrated by the questions you have. The ability to know Jesus isn't just available to some people, but to anyone who draws close to Him (James 4:8). However, once you have your answer, be prepared for changes in how you think, respond, and live.

If prayer and Bible reading are how you talk with God, then questions should be part of the dialogue. Don't be surprised if there are times when He asks you questions. He likes answers, too.

God, I've had some questions for years, but I've been
afraid to ask them. Give me the courage to ask,
expecting that You have the answers.

TRUSTING GOD TO ACT

Wait for the Lord; be strong and take heart and wait for the Lord.

PSALM 27:14 NIV

There will be times when you're incapable of changing a desperate situation. Then you must wait for God to act. Often, it takes great faith to believe that He's with you. It might seem like He has turned away. Isaiah said, "I will wait on the LORD, who hides His face from the house of Jacob; and I will hope in Him" (Isaiah 8:17 NKJV).

If you've disobeyed the Lord, He probably *has* turned His face away and isn't listening to your prayers (see Isaiah 59:1–2). But if you've repented, then you can have confidence that God loves you and will act.

You might go through a time of testing like Job, who was convinced for several months that God was against him. During such periods, you must trust God's Word and believe that "the mercy of the LORD is from everlasting to everlasting upon them that fear him" (Psalm 103:17 KJV). God is good and He will eventually come through for you.

*Dear Father, I repent of sins that have come between us.
Turn Your face back to me, O Lord! Give me the faith to believe
that You love me, and the patience to wait for You to act.*

JESUS CHRIST IS GREATER

But in these last days [God the Father] has spoken to us
by his Son, whom he appointed heir of all things.

HEBREWS 1:2 NIV

The more you worship Jesus Christ, the greater He will become in your eyes.

C. S. Lewis portrays the Christian's experience in book 2 of the Chronicles of Narnia. Lucy sees the lion Aslan—a Christ figure—shining white and huge in the moonlight. When she remarks that he's bigger, Aslan replies, "I am not. But every year you grow, you will find me bigger."

In Hebrews 1:2–3, Jesus Christ is honored (made bigger) in four ways in relation to God the Father. Let's consider two of the ways.

1. As the unique Son of God. By putting your trust in Christ, you become a son of God, His son, part of His family. But Jesus alone is God the Son.

2. As the heir of God. God has "appointed [Jesus] heir of all things." All things means *you* are part of His inheritance, *now and forever.*

No wonder you should worship and sing His praises!

Jesus, the better I know You, the greater I understand You
to be. I worship You as the unique and only Son of God,
who made all things and to whom all things belong.

JESUS CHRIST IS FULLY GOD

The Son is the radiance of God's glory and the exact
representation of his being.

HEBREWS 1:3 NIV

Jesus Christ was God entering fully into humanity—being supernaturally conceived, naturally formed in His mother's womb, and born into humble circumstances.

In Hebrews 1:2-3, God the Son is honored in four ways in relation to God the Father. Let's consider the third and fourth ways.

3. As the manifestation of God. Jesus is "the radiance of God's glory." The phrase speaks of a flood of resplendent light. The word *radiance* means an outshining, not a reflection.

As the brilliance of the sun is inseparable from the sun itself, so the Son's radiance is inseparable from the Deity.

4. As the revealer of God. The phrase "the exact representation of his being" reiterates that Jesus Christ is fully God—equal to and yet distinct from God the Father.

One encounter with God's Son is enough to change someone forever. What was your most profound experience with Him?

Jesus, You are God, and I worship You! Thank You for revealing
Yourself in Your Word and for giving me a personal
revelation of who You are.

THE INDWELLING WORD

Let the word of Christ dwell in you richly.

COLOSSIANS 3:16 NKJV

"When I discovered your words, I devoured them. They are my joy and my heart's delight" (Jeremiah 15:16 NLT). How can you *eat* God's Word? You do this by taking it into your heart, meditating on it, absorbing it, and allowing it to give you life. Just as you must chew, swallow, and digest natural food, so you must take God's Word into your being.

Paul wrote that you're to be "nourished in the words of faith and of the good doctrine which you have carefully followed" (1 Timothy 4:6 NKJV). You allow the word of Christ to nourish you when you make time to read it. This can be difficult to do in today's busy world. You may have so much to do that you feel you don't have time.

But failing to read the Bible is like failing to eat regular meals: you may get away with it for a little while, but eventually it will catch up with you. You'll feel weak. So take in a meal of scripture today.

Dear God, help me to eagerly devour Your Word. Help me to grasp that I can't survive without it—nor can I prosper or grow spiritually. In Jesus' name, I pray.

GOD LOOKS AT THE HEART

"Do not consider his appearance or his height, for I have rejected
him. The LORD does not look at the things people
look at. People look at the outward appearance,
but the LORD looks at the heart."

1 SAMUEL 16:7 NIV

What does a king look like? If you'd asked that question in David's day, you'd have heard a lot about personal appearance: height, muscular build, and even tone of voice. Even the prophet Samuel made the mistake of confusing a kingly bearing with competence. You, too, may assume that the person who looks the part is the best qualified.

God, however, looks at the heart. You shouldn't overlook the possibility that this passage applies to you as well. If you sense a potential call to serve in a place or capacity that feels beyond your abilities, God may be calling you to step out in faith.

The heart oriented toward God can accomplish far more than wisdom and experience can. If you feel unqualified for God's call, you're in very good company. In fact, God takes particular delight in using the supposedly "unqualified" to bless others.

Lord, may I not judge people, or even myself, by outward
criteria. May I look to You to show me who will work
best or what solution will work best.

WISDOM'S SOURCE

If any of you lacks wisdom, you should ask God, who gives
generously to all without finding fault, and it will be given to you.

JAMES 1:5 (NIV)

Wisdom is often equated with the number of wrinkles on a man's face. But wisdom comes from a place other than time alone. Wisdom most often comes from accepting God's Word as truth and living your life according to it. Proverbs 1:7 (NIV) affirms, "The fear of the LORD is the beginning of knowledge."

Too often you think you become wise by living through difficulties and learning a lesson afterward. That's a good source of common sense—and part of the reason older folks have so much good advice to share—but true wisdom from God offers *uncommon* sense, inspired instructions from the Creator Himself on how best to live and honor Him in His world.

Maybe those you say are "wise beyond their years" have simply been spending time learning wisdom from its true source. Don't let age fool you. Wisdom is available to all, and godly wisdom surpasses the earthly wisdom of anyone you know.

Dear Lord, I ask You for wisdom to deal with life's many
problems. You said all I had to do was ask, so I'm asking.
Help me to recognize Your wisdom when it comes.

CRYING AND LAUGHING

*To every thing there is a season, and a time to every purpose
under the heaven. . .a time to weep, and a time to laugh.*

ECCLESIASTES 3:1, 4 KJV

As you look through the Bible, you see again and again that men
of God weren't afraid to show their emotions. From Jacob and
Esau weeping as they embraced to King David publicly lamenting
Absalom, his son, Bible men often wept.

And they just as frequently laughed. They even had a proverb:
"A feast is *made* for laughter" (Ecclesiastes 10:19 KJV, emphasis
added), so they looked forward to times when they could cut loose
and laugh. During the course of your life, you can expect both
sorrow and joy, times that are enough to make a grown man cry
as well as others that cause laughter.

Many men wish that they could have *only* happy times, an
"abundant life" in which they never experience stress, hardship,
or sorrow. But this is an unrealistic expectation. Thank God for
the happy times. Enjoy them to the full. Know that you'll also
experience times of sorrow—but remember that you won't have
to walk them alone.

*God, thank You for happy occasions, funny moments, and times
of relaxing with family and friends. Help me also
through the sad times and the sorrows.*

GOD'S PURPOSE FOR LIFE'S TRIALS

Consider it pure joy, my brothers and sisters, whenever you face trials of many kinds, because you know that the testing of your faith produces perseverance.

JAMES 1:2-3 NIV

Albert Einstein once made an insightful observation about dealing with life's difficulties when he said, "Adversity introduces a man to himself." When life brings difficulties your way, you see where you're really at in your walk with God.

The Lord never promised His people an easy ride. In fact, the Bible is very clear—in many passages—that trials, storms, and suffering will be part of every believer's life. If you don't believe that, just take a look at the lives of the apostles, the men Jesus chose to take His message of salvation to the world. Nearly all of them experienced imprisonment, beatings, even martyrdom.

God also doesn't automatically make you a patient person once you're saved, and He doesn't instantly make you a person of great perseverance, either. Instead, He uses a process where the trials in your life strengthen you and make you the patient, persevering man He intends for you to be.

Dear God, help me to be patient and to persevere despite difficulties. I tend to be impatient, prone to giving up. Help me. Strengthen me, O God, I pray!

WHO'S LOOKING OUT FOR ME?

I know, GOD, that mere mortals can't run their own lives, that men and women don't have what it takes to take charge of life.

JEREMIAH 10:23 MSG

Humans are prone to wander, make mistakes, and become defeated. Earth's first couple had very simple rules to follow. However, it seemed easy for them to believe that God was holding all the best for Himself and that following Him wasn't in their best interest.

You're probably no different. You may feel God doesn't really understand you. You may believe He will withhold something you want.

God designed you to embrace His plan and purpose, but because of sin, your natural bent is to look out for yourself. You can be convinced that things, fame, and money provide a path to the satisfaction you want, but they don't. Instead, the self-centered pursuit of these things pulls you away from God, the only One who can truly satisfy you.

A self-focused lifestyle often leads to misunderstanding, to misapplication of what you learn, and to misguided trips to places God has marked KEEP OUT! In what parts of life have you been only looking out for yourself?

Lord, help me to trust You, to be convinced that You're not withholding anything from me but will work out Your plan in my life in due time.

DON'T LOSE YOUR CROWN

*"Hold on to what you have, so that no one
will take away your crown."*

REVELATION 3:11 NLT

James said, "Blessed is the man who. . .will receive the crown of life which the Lord has promised to those who love Him" (James 1:12 NKJV). This crown symbolizes your salvation and is God's gift to you.

Elsewhere, Peter says, "You will receive the crown of glory that will never fade away" (1 Peter 5:4 NIV). Many Bible scholars believe the crown of glory is *separate* from the crown of life. Can someone have more than one crown? Jesus does. "On his head were many crowns" (Revelation 19:12 KJV).

When promising "the crown of glory," Peter was talking to mature Christians who watched over the church. The crown of life is given to *all* believers, but the crown of glory is an award for exceptional service.

If God has given you a task to do and you fail to do it, He will have to find someone else to do it. . .and they will receive your reward (Revelation 3:11). So be faithful to fulfill your calling.

*God, thank You for my salvation, which is secure in You.
I pray You help me to be faithful to fulfill my calling,
the job You've given me to do.*

LEAVING HOME

When Jacob learned that there was grain in Egypt, he said to his sons, "Why do you just keep looking at each other?"
GENESIS 42:1 NIV

● ● ●

It's easy to identify with Jacob's frustration. Caught in a great famine, he felt the specter of starvation loom over his family. But his sons sat around looking at each other as if they didn't know what to do. Many people are more like Jacob's sons than Jacob. They're comfortable where they are, and when faced with a long and difficult journey, would rather stay home.

Like Jacob's family, however, you can't always find what you need where you are, especially if your relationship with Christ has become as dry as a desert and you're reluctant to move. You'll starve if you don't do what must be done. Ultimately, you know where to go to find what you need.

Embarking on a life-giving spiritual journey means leaving comfortable habits behind, enduring difficulties, and overcoming barriers. But the riches of the kingdom of God wait at the end of the journey.

Dear Lord, help me not to procrastinate, to keep putting off doing what needs to be done. Put some conviction in my spirit to make the changes to my life I need to make.

THE BREATH OF LIFE

*Then the LORD God formed a man from the dust of the ground
and breathed into his nostrils the breath of life,
and the man became a living being.*

GENESIS 2:7 NIV

Genesis 1 describes the origin of everything from a formless, dark void, culminating in the creation of man, made in God's likeness and given a purpose—to use his God-given qualities to complete the picture God had begun (Genesis 1:28).

But there's one important element to man's creation that makes him unique: God breathed life into him to make him a "living being [literally, *soul*]." And interestingly, this breath of life was into his "nostrils" rather than his mouth. The natural position of the mouth is closed, but the natural state of the nostrils is open.

Adam was designed to stay in connection with God in order to carry out his mission. Of course, willful disobedience ruined that plan. But hope returned with the promise of the Holy Spirit. In Christ, your connection to God through the Holy Spirit is as real, as essential, and as satisfying as the next breath you take.

*Father in heaven, thank You for creating me. I pray that
just as You gave me physical life, You will daily pour
Your Spirit into me and fill me with spiritual life.*

AVOID PRIDE OF ACCOMPLISHMENT

*I labored more abundantly than they all, yet not I,
but the grace of God which was with me.*

1 CORINTHIANS 15:10 NKJV

Jesus had told His apostles, "You shall be witnesses to Me in Jerusalem, and in all Judea and Samaria, and to the end of the earth" (Acts 1:8 NKJV). However, for the next twenty years, all twelve apostles remained in Jerusalem, content to preach in Judea and Samaria.

Paul, meanwhile, was going to far-flung cities across the Roman Empire. He wasn't exaggerating when he said, "I labored more abundantly than they all." But this didn't make Paul proud. He had just finished declaring, "I am the least of the apostles" (1 Corinthians 15:9 NKJV).

Paul was aware that God was using him to accomplish great things, but he also knew that it was the power of God changing lives—not him. And he was aware of his own unworthiness.

When you accomplish something great, don't put on false humility and say it's nothing. If it was praiseworthy, acknowledge the fact. But be sure to give the Lord the praise for using you.

---

*Lord, thank You for how You've used me. I don't take credit
for what has been accomplished. I know it was Your
Spirit guiding me, inspiring me, and empowering me.*

TROUBLE LETTING GO

"Let me kiss my father and mother goodbye,"
he said, "and then I will come with you."
1 KINGS 19:20 NIV

Elisha had trouble letting go (1 Kings 19:19–21). When the prophet Elijah made Elisha his successor, Elisha's first reaction was to go home and say good-bye to his parents.

His reaction is similar to those who made excuses for not following Christ. In His parable of the great banquet (Luke 14:15–23), Jesus recounted three things people had trouble releasing. The first man bought land and needed to see it. He couldn't let go of his *place*. The second man bought oxen and had to see them. He couldn't let go of his *possessions*. The third man wanted to be with his new wife. He couldn't let go of *people*.

Elisha and the characters in Christ's parable had the opportunity for a new life. But the stories end differently. Elisha severed the ties to his past and went after his future. The characters in Christ's parable wouldn't let go. They lost the opportunity.

We need empty hands to take up our cross and follow Him (Mark 8:34–38).

God, may I not cling to places, possessions, or people
but follow You wholeheartedly. Help me to let go of things
that would prevent me from living for You.

CATCH GOLD FEVER

The decrees of the LORD....are more precious
than gold, than much pure gold.
PSALM 19:9–10 NIV

It has been said that during the California gold rush in the 1800s the only people really making money were the business owners selling mining equipment and food. There were lots of glassy-eyed adventurers who would trade a large sum of gold for better shovels, picks, lanterns, pans, and a bag of flour or sugar.

There weren't any online shops where these miners could compare prices. They were forced to either live with what they had or pay the high store prices in the hopes of earning even more gold with their new tools. Some lost their lives in the mines, many stopped thinking clearly, and others left their claims broken and penniless.

When gold fever hit, these miners were willing to give up everything to get the gold. They sought what they viewed as precious to the exclusion of almost every other pursuit.

If God's Word is more precious than gold, it would seem you should have a great hunger (gold fever, if you will) to follow after God and what He has said.

Dear Lord, help me to be wholehearted and focused
on seeking the truth, both in Your Word and
in personal experience with You in prayer.

FREED TO SERVE

"I, the LORD, have called you in righteousness; I will. . .make you to be. . .a light for the Gentiles, to open eyes that are blind, to free captives from prison and to release from the dungeon those who sit in darkness."

ISAIAH 42:6–7 NIV

You know that God has made you righteous and freed you from sin's power, but are you freed from sin only for your own benefit? No. You have been freed in order to liberate others. But if you don't know where to start, there's good news.

The life of God is taking hold in you and reshaping your heart, desires, and thoughts. As God brings you liberty, you'll desire to share it with others. You'll begin to recognize the opportunities to share the light with those who are in darkness or to bring freedom to those who are trapped.

Perhaps the thing holding you back is doubt that God is with you and leading you. Are you open to His guidance? Do you need to set aside time today to allow His renewal to take hold in your life?

God, please give me faith that just as You broke my chains, You want to use me to help set others free. Help me to seize any opportunities You send me.

CONFIDENT IN CHRIST

*In him and through faith in him we may approach
God with freedom and confidence.*

EPHESIANS 3:12 NIV

So often when men pray to God for a pressing need, a sense of sinfulness rises up to discourage them: *You're unworthy. God won't answer your prayers. You might as well stop praying.* This is the voice of the enemy. His name, Satan, means "accuser" in Hebrew, and the Bible calls him "the accuser of our brethren" (Revelation 12:10 NKJV). He accuses *all* believers.

If you've given your heart to Christ, God has forgiven you. If there's current sin that you haven't repented of, however, it will hinder God from blessing you in this life (Isaiah 59:1–2).

But know this: God *will* forgive you as you confess your failings to Him (1 John 1:9). The devil may try to tell you that God won't forgive—but don't listen to that lie! God *does* forgive. "Let us therefore come boldly to the throne of grace, that you may obtain mercy and find grace to help in time of need" (Hebrews 4:16 NKJV).

*Father, I come to You for mercy. I ask You to forgive my sins
and give me the confidence that when I pray, You will
hear and answer. In Jesus' name, I ask. Amen.*

SECOND THOUGHTS

"We can't attack those people; they are stronger than we are."
NUMBERS 13:31 NIV

Moses sent twelve spies into Canaan in preparation for the coming invasion. But on the threshold of their greatest exploits, ten spies took a long, hard look at the challenges and decided they weren't worth it. They preferred their nomadic life to the battles before them. So those ten died in the desert. Only two of the spies reached the Promised Land.

Every man faces moments when the likelihood of success seems small, the obstacles seem insurmountable, and the costs seem immeasurable. Those who turn back never fulfill their dreams. Those who press on may fail, but at least they fail daring greatly.

On the threshold of a great accomplishment, of leaving behind the desert of this world and pursuing a glorious life in God, some turn back and refuse to step into new life. They're afraid. It costs too much. Victory seems impossible.

But those who refuse to retreat press on, live an adventure of faith, and follow God into the promised land of a full life. Will you live by fear or faith?

*God, please help me not to lose courage before life's battles
and turn back. Give me faith to believe that
You'll be with me and help me.*

THE RISKS OF RETURNING

Then Orpah kissed her mother-in-law goodbye.
RUTH 1:14 NIV

Orpah and Ruth faced the same choice—to go with Naomi to a new land and life or go back to Moab and the life they knew. Orpah refused new life. She followed Naomi's advice (Ruth 1:11–13) and went home, married, raised a family, and lived the rest of her days in Moab.

Ruth, however, lived an incredible life that far surpassed anything she could have imagined. She was David's great-grandmother and an ancestor of the Messiah. None of that could have happened without leaving Moab.

Ruth committed herself to God, to His people, and to their future without reservation. It was a long walk into a new land and a new life, but nothing could dissuade her. She had the strength to follow God regardless of what came her way. You see this same attitude in Jesus. "As the time approached for him to be taken up to heaven, Jesus resolutely set out for Jerusalem" (Luke 9:51 NIV).

Pursuing the hero's journey, the great adventure of faith, means leaving behind the life you have for the life you want. It's the only way.

Dear Lord, help me to have the faith and courage, like Ruth, to leave the familiar and the comfortable to follow You day by day.

A LIVING SACRIFICE

*I plead with you to give your bodies to God because of all he
has done for you. Let them be a living and holy sacrifice.*

ROMANS 12:1 NLT

Romans 12:1 describes laying yourself down as a "living sacrifice,"
and that might worry you since another verse says, "Those who
are Christ's have crucified the flesh with its passions and desires"
(Galatians 5:24 NKJV). You might think that following Jesus is
void of fun.

Certainly you'll need to make sacrifices out of love for God
and others, and certainly you shouldn't give in to sinful desires,
but you have many desires that are perfectly in line with God's
will. That's why He promises, "Delight yourself also in the LORD,
and He shall give you the desires of your heart" (Psalm 37:4 NKJV).

Let the Holy Spirit have His way. Listen when He tells you to
say no to a selfish desire, or urges you to crucify hatred, jealousy,
and covetousness. He wants what's best for you, and though you'll
die to sinful passions and lusts, you'll be truly coming alive.

*Father in heaven, help me to crucify my sinful tendencies,
to yield myself to You, so that You can give me the
things You long for me to have.*

PEACE BEYOND CIRCUMSTANCES

*"But the Advocate, the Holy Spirit, whom the Father will send
in my name, will teach you all things and will remind
you of everything I have said to you."*

JOHN 14:26 NIV

Jesus promised to send the Holy Spirit to comfort and instruct
His followers. Even after Jesus' resurrection, they still needed the
Spirit's peace.

You may think they had one more reason to be alarmed after
Jesus ascended to heaven...apparently abandoning them. However,
Jesus assured them that it was the exact opposite: because He
would send them the Spirit, they didn't need to fear.

Jesus assures you that you can have the guidance, wisdom,
and peace of the Holy Spirit when you too face situations where
fear appears to be warranted.

This isn't a guarantee that all your problems will be resolved
or that you'll suddenly have incredible wisdom to make choices.
Rather, the Spirit will assure you that you're not alone and that
whatever may happen, God remains with you. The Spirit guards
your soul and keeps you close to Jesus.

*Thank You, Jesus, for sending the Holy Spirit to dwell within me,
to comfort me, to lead me, and to reveal the truth to me.
May I always submit to and listen to Him.*

THE RIGHT THING TO BRAG ON

"Let not the wise boast of their wisdom or the strong boast of their strength or the rich boast of their riches, but let the one who boasts boast about this: that they. . .know me."

JEREMIAH 9:23-24 NIV

If you've ever been around someone who spends a lot of time bragging about his possessions, accomplishments, or talents, then you probably know why God isn't pleased with pride. An arrogant attitude can really irk you, and it doesn't take long.

When you boast about your own accomplishments, about your talents and gifts, you communicate that what you have and what you can do are a result of your own efforts, not a result of God's blessings. But He's the One who created you and gave you your abilities.

God doesn't want His people having an attitude of braggadocio. God wants you to make sure your words—especially those related to your gifts, blessings, and accomplishments—point to Him as your benefactor. And, as the verse above instructs, that should begin with the fact that you know Him as your loving heavenly Father.

Lord, help me to have a humble attitude, knowing that all my abilities and talents come from You. Help me to continually glorify You before others.

LIVING WHAT YOU UNDERSTAND

To him who knows to do good and does not do it, to him it is sin.
JAMES 4:17 NKJV

There are sins of omission as well as sins of commission. How often do men fail to do something good out of lethargy or simply a lack of concern? Solomon instructed, "Do not withhold good from those to whom it is due, when it is in the power of your hand to do so" (Proverbs 3:27 NKJV).

The Bible's most important teachings are very plain. There's little that's puzzling about them. The problem, however, is that they can be difficult to obey. For example, many Christians are deeply bothered by Jesus' command, "Love your enemies" (Matthew 5:44 NKJV). They reason that He couldn't really have meant that literally. So they withhold love from people they don't like.

There are many complex situations where you won't *know* the correct thing to do. In hindsight, yes, you may see clearly what you should've done. Once you understand clearly what you ought to do, however, it's a sin if you don't follow through and do it.

God, help me to obey the Bible's plain, simple teachings,
even when it's difficult. Help me to truly be Your
disciple, loving You and obeying Your commands.

GOING BACK

Paul did not think it wise to take him,
because he had deserted them in Pamphylia.

ACTS 15:38 NIV

John Mark had quit. So Paul refused to let him join their second missionary journey (Acts 15:36–41). Mark wasn't the only one who gave up. Paul later wrote that "Demas, because he loved this world, has deserted me" (2 Timothy 4:10 NIV).

Faced with the opportunity to journey into new and unknown territory, some refuse to go. They love the life they have too much to risk losing it. You know what that's like. You, too, have probably spent much time and effort creating the life you want. Once you get it, you don't want to change. Change is hard work and uncertain.

The sad story of Demas gives clear insight. His affections hadn't changed. He never stopped loving "this present world" with its comforts. He loved the world more than he loved the Lord, God's will for his life, and his calling in Christ. What he loved drove his behavior and led him to resist change.

So, what do *you* love most?

Lord, help me not to desert the high calling You have
given me. Help me to be willing to forsake the comforts
and security of my feathered nest and follow You.

SPEAKING JOYFULLY

He put a new song in my mouth, a hymn of praise to our God.

PSALM 40:3 NIV

Jesus has promised you abundant life here on earth as well as an eternity in paradise. He has promised you joy, both in this life and in the next. Those who follow Him have more reason than anyone to think thoughts and speak words that reflect joy.

But do you know a professing believer who always seems to be complaining, a person who, on the outside anyway, seems mostly devoid of the joy of the Lord? Or are *you* yourself sometimes that kind of Christian?

The Bible is filled with examples of men whose life situations weren't exactly reasons for happy or joyful attitudes. But instead of spending their time moaning, they focused on what God was doing in and through them—and they meditated on their eternal rewards. Even when life throws difficulty and suffering your way, you can have God's joy fill you so that you can't help but let it out when you speak.

Lord, thank You for saving me. Thank You for giving me the tremendous hope of heaven. Thank You for supplying my needs day after day. I praise You for Your goodness, God!

COMPANIONS ON YOUR JOURNEY

Then all the disciples deserted him and fled.

MATTHEW 26:56 NIV

John was at the cross the day Christ died (John 19:26–27). Judas had taken his own life (Matthew 27:3–5). But where were the other disciples? No one knows for sure.

Their desertion of Christ in Gethsemane isn't hard to understand. Running from danger is a natural response. You'd just like to think you would have done better.

But this illustrates two truths about your spiritual journey. First, you need friends with you. Jesus "appointed twelve that they might be with him" (Mark 3:14). For three years, they accompanied Him. When His crisis approached, He wanted them close and praying. He said to them, "Sit here while I go over there and pray" (Matthew 26:36 NIV).

Second, there are places others can't or won't go with you. There are trials you must face alone. But that doesn't mean you're truly alone. God is with you, even when you don't feel Him.

You need a band of brothers. But you also need the strength to pursue your journey whether or not they go with you.

God, help me to be a faithful friend to men walking a difficult road. May I pray for them and encourage them as I would like them to do for me.

CONTROLLING YOUR EYES

*"I made a covenant with my eyes not to
look with lust at a young woman."*
JOB 31:1 NLT

Job lived during an era when polygamy was acceptable, yet he was satisfied with *one* woman. Maybe it helped that she was exceptionally lovely, but still, Job realized that unless he determined ahead of time not to look lustfully at other women, his eyes would naturally wander. So he made a commitment *not* to allow his eyes to linger. Then, when faced with temptation, he refused to lust.

In modern times, men are constantly bombarded with sexually provocative sights. Even if you don't go looking for them, they can ambush you. If you haven't given thought to the matter ahead of time and determined your reaction, you almost can't help but gawk. But it can be very habit-forming and addictive.

The secret to victory is to gain control of your thoughts *beforehand* and determine not to look in lust, even if a woman tempts you. "Do not lust in your heart after her beauty or let her captivate you with her eyes" (Proverbs 6:25 NIV). Look away, if necessary. Ask God to help you.

*Dear God, help me to resolve not to look at a woman in lust.
Give me the inner strength I need to resist
temptations today and all days.*

A TIME TO UNITE

In Christ's family there can be no division into Jew and non-Jew,
slave and free, male and female. Among us you are all equal.
That is, we are all in a common relationship with Jesus Christ.
GALATIANS 3:28–29 MSG

Of all people on earth, Christians should remove racial discrim-
ination from their thoughts, yet some Christians struggle to embrace this truth: God doesn't discriminate based on the color of
a person's skin. Yet believers often divide themselves from each
other based on how much money they make, where they live, or
even their ethnic heritage.

Jesus' sacrifice was for *all* mankind. He said He brought
salvation to the Jew *and* the Gentile. That's *everyone*. He even loved
the Samaritans, an ethnic and religious group that the Jews called
"half-breeds" and went out of their way to avoid. As in everything,
Jesus is your example of how to live and love.

Jesus said His love was for the entire world, and He didn't
make any exceptions. Why should you? God has a family—and
when you don't exclude people, it's larger than you think.

God, help me to love others the way You love them,
the way Your Son loved people when He was on earth.
Help me to love all of the people You've created.

PEACE IS YOURS TODAY

God in all his fullness was pleased to live in Christ,
and through him God reconciled everything to himself.
He made peace with everything in heaven and on
earth by means of Christ's blood on the cross.

COLOSSIANS 1:19-20 NLT

How would you describe your mental state right now? Are you content or discouraged? Do you feel close to God or distant from Him? There may be times when you wonder if you'll ever be "good enough." But God has reconciled everything to Himself.

God is not distant from you. Jesus has come to dwell in you, and through the cross He demonstrated once and for all that He's fully committed to making peace with you. Any barriers between you and God have been removed. There is no way to make yourself worthier of the cross. Reconciliation has been accomplished.

You also have good news to share with others. The cross is for everyone on earth. You'll only be able to share that message if you first believe that God has made peace with you.

Heavenly Father, help me to trust that You've made complete
peace between me and You by the blood of Jesus Christ,
Your Son. Help me never to doubt that, I pray.

FORGIVING OTHERS: GOD REQUIRES IT

"And when you stand praying, if you hold anything against anyone, forgive them, so that your Father in heaven may forgive you your sins."

MARK 11:25 NIV

If you've been around someone who harbors bitterness toward another, you know how uncomfortable it can be. Anger and unforgiveness are like love and faith in that they always find outward expressions. You can't be an angry, bitter person without those around you seeing it in you—or hearing it from your mouth.

God, it turns out, takes forgiving others very seriously—so seriously that Jesus instructed His followers to forgive one another from their hearts. Otherwise, He said, God would not hear their prayers.

Have you ever been at a place in your relationship with God where your prayers seemed stale, where it seemed like they weren't reaching God's ears? There could be a lot of reasons for that—hidden sin, a spiritual struggle, and even those "dry times" you sometimes experience. But it's wise to examine your relationships with others and ask if you're harboring unforgiveness toward someone.

Then forgive. . .from your heart.

God, help me to deal with any failure to forgive. Help me to let go of bitterness I hold toward anyone and to completely and freely forgive them.

GODLY PURSUITS

But you, O man of God, flee these things [love of money
and empty pursuits] and pursue righteousness,
godliness, faith, love, patience, gentleness.
1 TIMOTHY 6:11 NKJV

When the Bible tells you to flee sin, it tells you to do so by pursuing new practices (Ephesians 4:21–24). In the verse above, Paul warned young Timothy about the perils of loving money. Then he told him to pursue righteousness, godliness, faith, love, patience, and gentleness.

What exactly does that look like? Pursuing righteousness isn't about hanging on to your salvation; rather, it's about dealing with one another justly. Pursuing godliness means doing your part in the sanctification process. You can do nothing to purify yourself of sin, but you *can* pray and read the Word.

Pursuing faith is about taking your eyes off your circumstances and focusing on God. Pursuing patience means bearing with loss, injury, and persecution. And pursuing gentleness means being kind and considerate toward others.

If the love of money is strong in you, the list of pursuits above is the antidote. As you begin to pursue them, you'll see spiritual victories in your life.

God, please help me pursue all these virtues listed here, and as I do that, fill me with Your Spirit and Your love. In Jesus' name, I pray.

HUSBANDS AND WIVES

There is neither Jew nor Greek. . .there is neither male
nor female: for ye are all one in Christ Jesus.
GALATIANS 3:28 KJV

The Declaration of Independence states "that all men are created equal, that they are endowed by their Creator with certain unalienable rights." You understand, of course, that when it states "all men," that it means "mankind"; it's self-evident that women have unalienable rights also.

The Bible shows the attitude that men should have when it says, "You husbands must give honor to your wives. Treat your wife with understanding as you live together. She may be weaker than you are, but she is your equal partner in God's gift of new life. Treat her as you should so your prayers will not be hindered" (1 Peter 3:7 NLT).

If your prayers are frequently being hindered, you might want to make sure you're honoring your wife. She isn't always right, any more than you are, but listen to her counsel, even as Manoah listened to his wife (Judges 13:21–23). Chances are good you'll be blessed and even learn something.

Lord God, please give me the wisdom and humility to listen
to my wife. Help me to treat her as I should
and to honor her. In Jesus' name, I pray.

BREAD FROM HEAVEN

*"You are looking for me, not because you saw the signs I
performed but because you ate the loaves and had your
fill."... So they asked him, "What sign then will you give
that we may see it and believe you? What will you do?
Our ancestors ate the manna in the wilderness...."*

JOHN 6:26, 30-31 NIV

Five thousand people knew a prophet was among them when the
baskets of food were being passed around (John 6:14). But as soon
as they were hungry again, the gift rather than the Giver became
their focus.

Though Jesus pointed this out, they tried to get Him to prove
Himself again by providing a daily supply of bread. Wouldn't that
be great? No more work, just collect free bread every day. They
hungered for an easy solution to life's hardships, not for Christ to
fill their souls.

It's like being hired to follow—*As long as I'm being paid, I'm
on God's side.* Let's not seek to be filled by God only for a day. He
offers so much more.

*Lord, You know I need "daily bread," and You even told me
to pray for it. But help me to seek "the Bread of Life"—
Your presence and Word—first and foremost.*

HARVEST UNDERSTANDING

See how the farmer waits for the land to yield its valuable crop, patiently waiting for the autumn and spring rains.

JAMES 5:7 NIV

Travel enough through the country and you'll see lots of farms and endless rows of corn, wheat, and beans. You'll see cattle, sheep, and horses. You'll pass trucks and tractors on dirt roads. Even in the biggest cities you'll find farmers' markets where the products farmers grow are on display and on sale.

Because people need to eat, there will always be a need for farmers. These are the men and women who plant and harvest the food you take for granted.

Jesus was very familiar with farming, and He used this culture to help share many truths. His agricultural parables illustrated lessons from spiritual growth to bad influences, from the way you listen to where you place your trust.

Jesus knew that farming-based teachings were a perfect way to help people learn more about the Christian life. Beyond the impact it has on the economy and your personal well-being, understanding farming can enhance your understanding of Jesus.

Lord, I'm truly grateful for the farmers who grow the food I eat. Bless them today. And bless my understanding of Your farming-related teachings and parables in the Bible.

GOD WANTS TO FORGIVE YOU

*Who is a God like you, who pardons sin and forgives
the transgression...? You do not stay angry
forever but delight to show mercy.*

MICAH 7:18 NIV

What do you imagine about God after you've sinned? Do you imagine an angry God, quick to turn you away? Do you imagine Him as indignant that you've failed again?

Whether you're struggling with habitual sin or you worry that your past transgressions are beyond God's forgiveness, He's more merciful than you can imagine. Micah compares the Lord to the false gods of his day—and assures you that God is completely unlike them.

Yes, sin is serious and can alienate you from God, but if you confess your sins, He is quick to forgive and restore you. Do you imagine God towering over you to strike you with judgment? Don't. The Bible assures you that His anger passes quickly and that He delights in mercy.

God takes no pleasure in judgment. If you want to delight Him, stop hiding your sins and failures. Bring them out before Him in plain sight and forsake them, so He can show mercy to you.

*God, I've messed up again, sinned again—just when I thought
I was doing better. I ask You to forgive me
and draw me close to You again.*

HOW YOU BRING JOY TO GOD

Let us continually offer the sacrifice of praise to God,
that is, the fruit of our lips, giving thanks to His name.
But do not forget to do good and to share, for with
such sacrifices God is well pleased.

HEBREWS 13:15–16 NKJV

The story of Jesus Christ, as God's eternal Son, has no beginning. The story of Christ as fully God *and* fully human begins with His conception and birth. And it ends with His sacrificial death on the cross and His resurrection three days later. But it actually didn't even end *there.* It was only fully complete when He sat down, triumphant, forty days later at the right hand of the Majesty on High.

So how do you worship Him? How do you show how much you love Him? You do so by praising God the Father, God the Son, and God the Holy Spirit with your mouth—both in prayer and in song. You also do so by doing good and sharing with others, "for with such sacrifices God is well pleased." Your words praising Jesus, and your good words and actions toward the people around you, bring God joy!

Lord, help me to worship and praise You with all my being—with
my thoughts, my words, and my actions! In Jesus' name, I pray.

SPIRITUAL GARDENING

Now he who plants and he who waters are one, and each one
will receive his own reward according to his own labor.
1 CORINTHIANS 3:8 NKJV

If you've ever been around someone who can turn an ordinary conversation into a spiritual one with thought-provoking, spiritual questions or observations, then your own attempts at witnessing probably feel inadequate by comparison. For most of us, the ground often seems dry and not very receptive to the Gospel.

Some Christians are called to plant seeds, while others are called to pour a little water on those seeds to bring the Gospel to fruition. But the two aren't mutually exclusive. You can be a planter who waters on occasion or a waterer who plants on occasion. The good news is that both will receive a reward.

But the apostle Paul doesn't leave any room in this verse for not gardening in some fashion. Sitting idly by while others do all the work isn't an option. How is your gardening going? Which role do you gravitate toward? Do you seek out the unconverted or do you nurture new believers instead?

Dear Father, lead me to responsive souls, and give me the
love and the boldness to speak to them about the Gospel.
Anoint my mind with wisdom and my words with grace.

WORKPLACE HUMOR

Nor should there be obscenity, foolish talk or coarse joking,
which are out of place, but rather thanksgiving.
EPHESIANS 5:4 NIV

If you work in a business that constantly interacts with the public, the language you hear is apt to be clean and courteous. But there are many trades where cursing and off-color humor are common—where coworkers habitually use foul language and find crude sexual jokes funny.

It's important that you don't encourage their behavior. If you laugh politely to avoid offending them, they'll be emboldened to keep going. So let them know, without giving offense, that this isn't your type of humor. Simply refrain from smiling at their jokes. They'll get the point.

Of course, you have little control over their reaction. Some men will take the cue and turn down the volume around you. Others may mock you and your Christian faith. Don't be surprised. Peter says, "You have spent enough time in the past doing what pagans choose to do. . . . They are surprised that you do not join them. . . and they heap abuse on you" (1 Peter 4:3–4 NIV).

Whatever others do, continue to follow Christ with a clear conscience.

God, please give me strong convictions about obscenity
and off-color jokes. I pray that You also give me
wisdom when addressing this issue.

FLOURISHING

The righteous will flourish like a palm tree.

PSALM 92:12 NIV

In Psalm 92:12–15, the palm tree is a symbol of the spiritual life Christ made possible for all His followers. Like the palm, you can grow and live a fruitful life.

Jesus made it possible for you to flourish and live a joy-filled, meaningful life.

He made it possible for you to sink your roots deep in the spiritual soil of His presence. You're planted in the house of the Lord.

He made it possible for you to have a fruitful, productive life for as long as you live.

He made it possible to stay spiritually healthy, to stay green and growing.

He gave you reason to shout with joy and proclaim His righteousness, power, and glory!

But remember that you only "flourish in the courts of our God" (Psalm 92:13 NIV). You must draw your life and strength from a deep and nourishing relationship with Him. An uprooted plant doesn't produce fruit. Are you "rooted and built up in [Jesus]"? Do you "grow up into him in all things" (Ephesians 4:15 KJV)?

Jesus, help me to sink my roots down deep into the truth
of who You are and of Your power to save me.
May I become strong and fruitful in You.

STARVING FOR GOD

*He humbled you, causing you to hunger and then feeding you
with manna. . .to teach you that man does not live on bread
alone but on every word that comes from the mouth of the LORD.*
DEUTERONOMY 8:3 NIV

As the people of Israel journeyed through a barren landscape, you
can hardly blame them for worrying about what they would eat,
drink, or wear in such a bleak location. Gathering enough food for
an entire nation in a land without fields for agriculture or pasture
for flocks became a daily struggle for survival. How could so many
people survive forty days, let alone forty years, in such a desert?

While the Israelites surely considered the wilderness the
last place they wanted to be, the Lord wasted no time in using it
for a good purpose. This thirsty land was where they would learn
complete dependence on Him.

In part, the Lord used a difficult situation to teach His people
complete and total dependence. They couldn't do anything clever
or innovative enough to provide for themselves. Their only way
out was prayer, and their only resource was God's help.

*God, thank You for the valuable lessons You teach me,
even in my desperate situations and lacks. Help me to
hunger for Your Word more than anything else.*

A GODLY MENTOR

Barnabas took Mark and sailed for Cyprus.
ACTS 15:39 NIV

● ● ●

John Mark was fortunate. Barnabas took him under his wing and took him on a missionary journey. This created a rift with Paul, but Barnabas thought Mark was worth it. Years later Paul asked Timothy to bring Mark to him because he was "helpful to [him] in [his] ministry" (2 Timothy 4:11 NIV).

Clearly, Mark had changed! Barnabas was an excellent spiritual mentor. You, too, sometimes need help to overcome your fears and step into your future.

Barnabas believed in Mark's potential, and you also need people who believe in you. Plus, he was willing to invest. Barnabas had invested in Paul and saw *that* investment pay off, so he was willing to make an investment in Mark also. And Barnabas was experienced. He had been where John Mark needed to go and could show him the way. Finally, Barnabas was an encourager. Barnabas, which means "son of encouragement," was his nickname (Acts 4:36).

You, too, need someone who can point you in the right direction and encourage you on the way. And you need to do that for others also.

God, help me to find a godly mentor when I need one.
And help me to be a mentor and an encourager
to those who are new in the faith.

DON'T BE COVETOUS

Don't set your heart on anything that is your neighbor's.
EXODUS 20:17 MSG

Exodus 20:17 (NKJV) says, "You shall not covet. . .anything that is your neighbor's." But *covet* is a bit of an archaic word. What exactly does it mean? *The Message* translates this verse thus: "Don't set your heart on anything that is your neighbor's."

The dictionary defines *covet* this way: "To desire wrongfully, inordinately, or without due regard for the rights of others." Thus, if you covet your neighbor's wife, you'll eventually seek to commit adultery with her—ignoring the pain this causes her husband and their children.

If you covet your neighbor's wealth, you'll seek ways to get it from him—or coveting will cause you to be bitter that you don't have what he has. The Bible advises, "Keep your lives free from the love of money and be content with what you have" (Hebrews 13:5 NIV).

One day in heaven, God will abundantly compensate you for your present lack. That's why Jesus said, "Blessed are you who are poor, for yours is the kingdom of God" (Luke 6:20 NIV).

God, help me not to covet the things other people have.
Help me to be content with what I have, however
much or little that is. In Jesus' name, I pray.

THE ROAD TO RESURRECTION

They came to a place called Golgotha.
MATTHEW 27:33 NIV

◈ ◈ ◈

The road to resurrection runs through Golgotha. The road Christ walked that day was good for us. It wasn't "good" for Christ, who suffered physical, emotional, and spiritual agony that you can only imagine.

It wasn't the road He wanted to follow. We're told that "he fell with his face to the ground and prayed, 'My Father, if it is possible, may this cup be taken from me' " (Matthew 26:39 NIV). He would have preferred to fulfill His mission without taking the road to Golgotha. Probably, so would you.

But it doesn't work that way. The trials and suffering were the only way to gain salvation for mankind. And the challenges you face along the road to a deeper life in Christ are just as necessary to break your sinful will and drive you to greater intimacy with God.

Christ shows the way. He submitted and prayed, "Not as I will, but as you will" (Matthew 26:39 NIV). Don't refuse to submit, don't reject the way of the cross, or you'll miss out on a deep, beautiful relationship with Christ.

Father, help me to yield to Your will, even when it's difficult.
You know what's best for me, so I'll let You choose
my path and plan my future.

TRUE RIGHTEOUSNESS

"For I tell you that unless your righteousness surpasses that of the Pharisees and the teachers of the law, you will certainly not enter the kingdom of heaven."

MATTHEW 5:20 NIV

God had given His people many commandments in the Law, which, if obeyed, would create a just and compassionate society. He didn't give the Law simply to burden His people with a plethora of rules. At the very heart of the Law were two commands: to love the Lord with all their hearts, and to love their fellow man as they loved themselves. If they obeyed these two commands, all the rest would follow.

The Pharisees and scribes, however, lost sight of this and focused on a legalistic adherence to the Law—and this inevitably morphed into a loveless, outward show, done for the benefit of onlookers. Worse yet, they added multitudes of their own rules, regulations, and traditions, demanding that people obey these, too.

However, the Law was impossible to keep perfectly. In fact, Jesus was the only man who obeyed God in all things. And if you accept His atoning death on the cross, you partake of His righteousness.

Lord Jesus, You were the only one who was ever truly righteous. Help me to trust in Your righteousness, not my own. Only You can save me!

GIVING GENEROUSLY *AND* WISELY

Give freely and spontaneously. Don't have a stingy heart.
DEUTERONOMY 15:10 MSG

Often it seems contrary to sound reason to give "freely and spontaneously." Aren't you supposed to follow a budget and not deviate from it with impulse purchases? Yes, but God makes a difference between selfish personal expenditures and unselfish giving.

However, some people have so *much* empathy that they would give away their car or drain their bank account. Remember, "wisdom brings success" (Ecclesiastes 10:10 NKJV). And bear in mind: you are to care for your family first (Matthew 15:5–6; 1 Timothy 5:8).

But there are times to give freely. The New King James Version states, "You shall surely give to him [the poor], and your heart should not be grieved when you give" (Deuteronomy 15:10). If you *know* that God wants you to give, then give—even if your natural reaction is to tightly clutch your hard-earned cash.

However, if you have reasonable doubts about whether it's wise to give, then don't. "Whatever is not from faith is sin" (Romans 14:23 NKJV).

*Lord, please give me both generosity and wisdom—
the generosity to be willing to give, and the wisdom
to know when to give and how much.*

SPEAKING A BLESSING

*All praise to God, the Father of our Lord Jesus Christ,
who has blessed us with every spiritual blessing in the
heavenly realms because we are united with Christ.*

EPHESIANS 1:3 NLT

Blessings are gifts from God. A blessing is also a personal gift a father shares with a child. A father's blessing can give a child permission to grow up experiencing love and security, and invite the child to dream big and follow God.

You pass the blessing on when you speak it. You can't assume your children understand they're loved and that you want the best for them. They need to hear it from your lips and see it in your actions. A blessing can change their future, strengthen their relationships, and provide a vision.

When children receive a blessing from their father, it proves he notices them, pays attention to them, and knows that by giving them wings they will eventually fly.

God has blessed mankind with a future and a hope. He offers a listening ear, a fully developed plan for your life, and eternal companionship. He advises, He comforts, and He *blesses*.

*Lord, help me to fervently love my children, pray for them,
and bless them in Your name. Help me to speak
continual blessings into their lives, I pray.*

OUT OF YOUR MIND

At this point Festus interrupted Paul's defense.
"You are out of your mind, Paul!"

ACTS 26:24 NIV

Saul of Tarsus, the brilliant Jewish rabbi, had abandoned a promising career to promote the hated sect he once wanted to destroy. When they heard Paul's story, King Agrippa and the Roman proconsul, Festus, thought he was insane. Paul stood before them and went on about dead men coming back to life and a heavenly vision—then tried to persuade them to join him (Acts 26)! No wonder Festus thought he was crazy and Agrippa was insulted.

Others may think great adventurers are out of their minds. But men with a vision want to do what others think can't be done, take journeys others deem impossible, follow the vision others can't see, and take risks others fear.

Deep in the heart of every man is an adventurer, a dreamer, and a hero. Like Paul, you long to follow the wild paths of a great vision. And, as with Paul, that journey begins as an encounter with the living Christ.

But don't be surprised if people say, "You're out of your mind!"

God, give me the vision and courage to strike off the beaten
path and follow You to great adventures. Give me the
courage to ignore the critics and naysayers.

PRACTICING HOSPITALITY

Dear friend, you are faithful in what you are doing for the brothers and sisters, even though they are strangers to you.
3 JOHN 1:5-6 NIV

Opening our homes to a missionary, minister, or fellow Christian is an important way to demonstrate the love of God. John noted that an elder named Gaius had recognized these ministers as brothers and sisters rather than as strangers. Gaius likely went to great lengths to host these traveling preachers in his home.

Inviting fellow Christians into your home, whether for a small group meeting, a family dinner, or lodging for several days, forces you to change your schedule, to share your resources, and to make space for others. If you truly believe that you are "brothers and sisters" with fellow Christians, the proof will be in how generously you share your home.

Hospitality is a sacrifice, but it's a vital way to encourage and support fellow believers. Along the way, you'll enjoy deeper relationships with your Christian family and even benefit from the blessings and prayers of those who share your home.

Lord, please help me to be generous and practice hospitality with needy fellow believers. For I know that in taking one of Your children into my home, I'm taking You in.

AVOID ARGUMENTS

*Refuse to get involved in inane discussions;
they always end up in fights. God's servant must not
be argumentative, but a gentle listener.*

2 TIMOTHY 2:23-24 MSG

If you're often drawn into arguments, you may simply think that you're "telling it like it is," or setting other people straight. But most quarrels create hard feelings and become emotional exchanges rather than reasoned discussions. Ask yourself what you spend the most time doing during an argument. Do you patiently listen to the other person, trying to understand his point of view, or does "listening" mean impatiently waiting for your turn to speak? The Bible says God's servant must be "a gentle listener."

Granted, there are times when you must "contend earnestly for the faith" (Jude 1:3 NKJV). But you must contend with facts and solid reasons, not with a raised voice and intimidating body postures.

Solomon said, "Starting a quarrel is like opening a floodgate, so stop before a dispute breaks out" (Proverbs 17:14 NLT). Know what's actually worth disputing and what's not. Often the wisest thing you can do is to avoid getting drawn into an argument.

---

*Lord, please forgive my pride and temper. They've caused
problems in my life, and I want to change. Please give me
love and patience. In Jesus' name, I pray. Amen.*

IT WON'T BE EASY

The crucible for silver and the furnace for gold,
but the LORD tests the heart.

PROVERBS 17:3 NIV

No one said getting from where you are to where you want to be in your walk with God is easy.

Jesus warned that you would have trouble in this world (John 16:33). James said you should rejoice in trials because of what they produce in you (James 1:2–4). Paul compared this life to harsh athletic discipline (1 Corinthians 9:24–27). Solomon compared it to gold in the refiner's fire (Proverbs 17:3).

When you pursue Christ with all your heart, you live a life that challenges the world around you and may prompt a hostile response. The world hates Him and all who follow Him. That draws you into spiritual warfare. Your enemy uses all his power to deceive you, block your way, and make sure you pay a high price for following God.

You often tend to run from and resent struggles. You want glory without the cross. But it never happens that way. No one said it would be easy. . .just worth it!

Dear God, I know You want the best for me, so purify me
as gold is melted in a furnace so that the impurities
can be scooped off. Help me to yield to Your process.

THE MAD GOLD RUSH

"Wisdom is more valuable than gold and crystal."
JOB 28:17 NLT

The California gold rush began on January 24, 1848. The next year, 1849, some three hundred thousand "forty-niners" rushed to California in hopes of striking it rich. It sounds exciting, but this was a dark period in America's history.

By 1855, when the madness ended, some 4,200 people had been murdered, 5,300 miners had starved or died without medicine, 1,400 people had committed suicide, 1,700 had gone insane, and 120,000 Native Americans had been wiped out. "The love of money is a root of all kinds of evil" (1 Timothy 6:10 NKJV).

You might have had the idea that rough-and-tumble events like the gold rush are what built our country. But the credit belongs elsewhere. During this same time, many Bible-believing pioneers traveled across America to claim a farm and patiently work the soil. For them, contentment and wisdom were the greatest riches.

"Greedy people try to get rich quick but don't realize they're headed for poverty" (Proverbs 28:22 NLT). Today, just like in the gold rush days, unselfishness, hard work, and patience turn out to be truly wise in the long run.

*Dear Father, help me to understand that eternal principles
and values are far more important than earthly riches.
Help me to grasp this deep within my heart.*

GOD NEVER GIVES UP

Finish what you started in me, GOD.
Your love is eternal—don't quit on me now.
PSALM 138:8 MSG

Do you ever feel panicked, watching the days of your life stretch out before you and not knowing how best to use them? If you've felt anything like that, take comfort in these truths:

- God is the author of your faith; He's writing your story (Hebrews 12:2).

- God is not a God of chaos. He's putting your life in order (1 Corinthians 14:33).

- God began a good work, and He'll complete it in you (Philippians 1:6).

- God saves through His power, grace, and love.

You always have access to the God who is reshaping your heart, reordering your direction, and giving purpose to your tomorrows.

God is faithful, and He won't give up on you. There will be moments when you're stubborn and unwilling to listen, but He won't throw up His hands in despair. He will wait for you, encourage you, and put detour signs in your path.

He can be trusted to do His part. While God does the work, life transformation will require your cooperation.

Lord, thank You for not giving up on me, even during times
when I drifted from You. Thank You for restoring me.

LIVING IN GOD

You are not controlled by your sinful nature. You are controlled by the Spirit if you have the Spirit of God living in you.

ROMANS 8:9 NLT

When you fail, you often simply try harder. You remind yourself that you know right from wrong, so all you need to do is police yourself and redouble your efforts. After all, God gave you His laws, so shouldn't it be easy to obey them?

But if you're like most men, you've become a master at riding the edge of sin and hoping you don't fall off the edge. All the self-discipline, all the good intentions have never been 100 percent successful in keeping you away from sin, because they're simply not enough.

God sent a Helper called the Holy Spirit to be both a companion and a guide. However, you often ignore His influence and advice. God wants to help you avoid sin, but you need to be willing to accept His help. Ask God to open your heart to the Spirit's leading, and ask the Spirit Himself what He would show you today.

God, I can only make it if I live my life in You.
Forgive me for trying to better myself through my own efforts.
Fill me with Your Spirit so I am guided daily by You.

A NETWORK OF FAITHFUL FRIENDS

"I commend to you. . ."

ROMANS 16:1–16 NIV

It's a stunning list.

At the end of his letter to the Romans, Paul takes time to greet, commend, and express gratitude to twenty-five individuals and, in some cases, their congregations. They were of great value to Paul's ministry. His accomplishments wouldn't have been possible without them.

It isn't just more difficult to make this journey alone. It's impossible. You need allies who will walk the road with you. You'll need help along the way. Paul's allies were his benefactors, his coworkers, and his friends. He even mentions that Rufus' mom had been a mother to him (Romans 16:13).

Also, each of these people supported and encouraged him on the way. Together they provided a network of material, emotional, and spiritual support. When Paul suffered, they comforted him. When Paul was discouraged, they encouraged him. Paul accomplished great things and reached great heights standing on their shoulders.

You need to build this kind of network and work at keeping these relationships strong. You simply can't "go it alone."

Lord, please help me to be a good friend to my friends, to support,
encourage, and invest time in them, as I wish them to do for me.

AVOID DRIFTING AWAY

We must pay the most careful attention. . .to what we
have heard, so that we do not drift away.

HEBREWS 2:1 NIV

Most people who leave faith in God don't make a sudden, deliberate decision to do so. Rather, they gradually become colder to the Lord; lose interest in praying, reading the Word, and fellowshipping with others; and, over time, value their relationship with God less and less.

Hebrews 2:3 (NIV) asks, "How shall we escape if we ignore so great a salvation?" But that's what many people do. They ignore God. Eventually they become "nearsighted and blind, forgetting that they have been cleansed from their past sins" (2 Peter 1:9 NIV). They often still go through the motions of being a Christian, but their heart is not in it. They question the basics of their faith and believe they're irrelevant to life in the modern world.

How can you avoid this? You must pay careful attention to what you have heard from the Bible. When you hear the Word, ponder it deeply and allow it to change you. Pray for God to renew your relationship with Him.

Dear God, keep me close to You, loving You, hungry for
Your Word and Your Spirit! Let me never drift away
from You. In Jesus' name, I ask. Amen.

NERVOUS, NERVOUS, NERVOUS

For what I received I passed on to you as of first importance:
that Christ died for our sins according to the Scriptures,
that he was buried, that he was raised on the
third day according to the Scriptures.

1 CORINTHIANS 15:3–4 NIV

You're God's ambassador. This means that people will hold God to whatever you say about Him. On top of that, if what you tell people about God is wrong, He isn't going to back it up. You'd better explain Him correctly, or God will hold you accountable. As will the world.

That's why the stories He asks you to tell are so breathtakingly simple. Whether it's the story of Jesus or your own story you tell others, they're both almost impossible to get wrong. Plus you have the Holy Spirit to back you up, to give your words power, and to prod you if you go off on some tangent.

And He has left you His Word, which tells of Jesus and what He did to save you, four times—in black and white. It's unmistakable. And surely you know your own testimony! This isn't metaphysics. There is little to be nervous about.

Lord, help me to accurately explain the Gospel message
to others, not giving the wrong impression,
but telling it plainly and simply.

GETTING READY

*And that you may love the L*ORD *your God,*
listen to his voice, and hold fast to him.

DEUTERONOMY 30:20 NIV

◈ ◈ ◈

The Israelites approached the greatest challenge of their lives, and Moses wanted them to be ready. We too will face great challenges, moments when it feels like a life or death situation.

Moses' instructions had nothing to do with being a conquering army and everything to do with having a right relationship with God. Strategies and techniques wouldn't have mattered if the Israelites hadn't been spiritually prepared. Moses gave four instructions (Deuteronomy 30:20):

First, love God. You will always follow your greatest love. If He's not your one great love, you will falter when asked to sacrifice for what you truly love.

Second, listen to God. God speaks to you through His Word, His Spirit, and His people. He will lead you if you follow His voice.

Third, link your life to His. You must take hold of God with an iron grip. He won't let go of you, but you must hold on to Him.

Finally, lean on His promises. God has made many promises. He will keep them, but you must keep faith in them.

Dear Lord, please give me a heart to love You. I want to listen
to You, to be united with You, and to trust in Your promises.

SURROUNDED BY TROUBLE

*"In this godless world you will continue to experience
difficulties. But take heart! I've conquered the world."*

JOHN 16:33 MSG

The Bible states that "man is born to trouble as surely as sparks fly upward" (Job 5:7 NIV). Jesus Himself promised that "in this world you will have trouble" (John 16:33 NIV). He literally guaranteed it, and it's just as likely to happen on one day as the next.

Many serious problems are caused by the unrelenting attacks of your spiritual enemy. In his hymn "A Mighty Fortress Is Our God," Martin Luther wrote that "our ancient foe doth seek to work us woe," but God is our helper "amid the flood of mortal ills." He ends with this triumphant declaration: "And though this world, with devils filled, should threaten to undo us, we will not fear, for God hath willed His truth to triumph through us."

So despite your troubles, take heart! Jesus has overcome the world, and despite every problem that Satan throws your way, God will eventually cause you to triumph. You may end up with a few dents, but God will come through. He won't abandon you.

*Father, thank You that You're with me, despite the flood
of mortal ills that seeks to sweep me away. Help me,
Lord! Make Your truth triumph through me.*

CHOICES AND CONSEQUENCES

"From everyone who has been given much,
much will be demanded."

LUKE 12:48 NIV

The more of God you experience, the more He expects of you. One of the barriers to greater spiritual life is failing to realize that God's call accompanies His joy. But why? Why aren't you free to just enjoy knowing God without the burden of service?

First, growing in God isn't only about you. It's also about God's glory in the world.

Second, growing in God prepares you to participate in His great work in the world. Your relationship with Him is precious. But God wants everyone to know that joy and has chosen you as His emissary.

Third, growing in God strengthens you for the inevitable challenges you will face. You know Him, and you know He will strengthen, sustain, and stay with you.

Finally, it's good for you. You were created to live on purpose for a great cause. You can't fulfill that destiny or know that satisfaction without a great mission.

What is God calling you to do?

Lord, I thank You for how You have blessed me,
taught me, and prepared me for the work You have for me.
Help me to rise up quickly and obey when You call.

HOW LONG HAS IT BEEN?

"As in the days when you came out of Egypt,
I will show them my wonders."
MICAH 7:15 NIV

● ● ●

The women know it's the right tomb. It has the same stone, though it's been moved. And that's the cloth that Jesus' body was bound in, blood and all. But suddenly two angels are there in lightning-bright garments. The women are stunned and amazed. Something unimaginable is happening. But the angels' message is simple: "Go tell His disciples."

Forty days later, Jesus is speaking, and a low cloud rolls down the slope—they'd seen it happen on these hills a thousand times—but then this cloud is blowing back up to the sky with Jesus on it, his hands outstretched. Then, while the disciples are overwhelmed by what they have just seen, two angels appear in bright garments and ask, "What are you doing standing here?"

How long has it been since God's wonders have left you speechless? Have you seen grace in the trust of a child, grandeur in a sunset, or breathtaking beauty in a forest? How long has it been since you were standing openmouthed with wonder?

God, thank You for the small wonders and miracles You show me, often day after day. Help me not to ignore those awe-filled moments. Reveal Yourself to me continually, I pray.

BREAKING FREE OF UNFORGIVENESS

*Forgive one another as quickly and thoroughly
as God in Christ forgave you.*

EPHESIANS 4:32 MSG

Who do you spend the most time thinking about? Those you love? Maybe, but there may be another group of people who fill your thoughts—sometimes daily: those who have hurt you.

You may replay their misdeeds over and over again. And often, the more you think about them, the angrier you get. The angrier you get, the more hurt you feel. The more hurt you feel, the more blame you place on the offender.

However, you can give forgiveness even when there's no apology—even when the offender never asks to be pardoned. However, forgiveness doesn't mean an automatic renewal of friendship or trust. You can forgive an offense, but if the offender doesn't change his behavior, he may not be brought into close confidence again.

You should forgive as God forgave you to prevent a "bitter root" from springing up in your heart (Hebrews 12:15 NIV). Are you willing to let go of the offenses you're holding on to?

*Dear God, please help me forgive those who have hurt me
or done me wrong. And give me wisdom as to how much
I should trust them. In Jesus' name, I pray. Amen.*

INVESTING IN GOD'S GIFT

Children are a gift from the LORD; they are a reward from him.
PSALM 127:3 NLT

God means for you to view parenting as a great privilege and an awesome responsibility. He doesn't want you to neglect the opportunities to invest in your kids, but to learn who they are, what interests them, and what communicates your love most effectively to them so you can teach them God's ways.

You should consider your role as a dad to be one of the most important responsibilities you'll ever have—or, if you're not a dad yet, ever will have. You can't take money, awards, or your favorite team jersey with you to heaven, but you can build relationships with your children that allow you to share your faith with them.

Jesus invited children to come to Him. As a dad, you too must gather your children into your arms and bless them. God describes His "reward" to you as a continuous relationship, not a onetime gift. Why? Your daily investments have a greater impact than one end-of-life award. Your children want ongoing quality time with you. Be determined to give it to them.

Lord, please show me how and when I can invest in each of my children's lives. Let them know clearly that I love them and that they're important to me.

PROSPERITY AND SUCCESS

"Keep this Book of the Law always on your lips; meditate on it day and night, so that you may be careful to do everything written in it. Then you will be prosperous and successful."

JOSHUA 1:8 NIV

● ● ●

Every man longs to be prosperous and successful in life. You, too, desire to have a meaningful occupation and to provide for your family. You want to live life for God and at the end hear Him say, "Well done, good and faithful servant!" (Matthew 25:21 NIV).

Joshua's desire to be prosperous and successful was no different from yours. And his stakes were desperately high. In addition to leading a family, he was also leading a nation into hostile territory. But the Lord gave him the formula for success: focus on God's Word, which will lead to a resolute trust in Him.

Don't miss this word to you: the *only* sure way to prosperity and success, as God defines it, is to faithfully read and follow His Word. He has provided the path with His promise of success in His Word. Follow that template, and you can be assured of success.

Lord, teach me what true success and prosperity are.
Give me the right focus in life so that I may please
You in all things and be truly blessed.

WORSHIP, SUBMIT, AND CONNECT

"Therefore go and make disciples of all nations."
MATTHEW 28:19 NIV

The disciples had seen Jesus crucified and raised from the dead, and they spent forty days with Him (Matthew 28:16–20; Mark 16:14-20). Their journey completely changed them—and your journey should change you.

"When they saw him, they worshiped him" (Matthew 28:17 NIV). Your spiritual journey should change what is of supreme value in your life. You may enjoy the things of this world, but you are no longer focused just on them.

" 'All authority in heaven and on earth has been given to me' " (Matthew 28:18 NIV). Christ is the authority, not you. You submit to Him and pursue His purposes.

" 'Surely I am with you always' " (Matthew 28:20 NIV). The sweetest result is your connection to Christ and His abiding presence with you.

"But some doubted" (Matthew 28:17 NIV). Seeing the resurrected Christ didn't convince all His disciples. You can expect some doubts and struggles to remain. They energize your pursuit of more of God. Doubts aren't failures. They're proof of your hunger for God!

God, I pray that You continually transform me so that You are of supreme value to me. May I pursue Your purposes and dwell in Your presence. In Jesus' name, I pray.

GETTING DISTRACTED

"While your servant was busy here and there,
the man disappeared."

1 Kings 20:40 niv

One day a prophet of God called out to King Ahab after a critical campaign and said, "Your servant went into the thick of the battle, and someone came to me with a captive and said, 'Guard this man. If he is missing, it will be your life for his life. . . .' While your servant was busy here and there, the man disappeared" (1 Kings 20:39–40 niv).

Many men have, at times, become so busy with a little here and there that they failed to focus on what was truly important. They allowed themselves to get sidetracked in nonessentials and before they knew it, they'd fiddled away their time.

You must cultivate the virtue of self-control (2 Peter 1:6 niv). Paul said that men must be "self-controlled. . .and disciplined" (Titus 1:8 niv). Even if you're bored with a task, put forth the effort to focus on it and finish it. Or even if you shy away from a responsibility because it's difficult or unpleasant, roll up your sleeves and do it. You'll be glad you did.

Lord, help me concentrate on the things I need to
accomplish and not let anything distract me.
Help me be diligent and faithful. Amen.

LOVING THE SINNER. . .

To others show mercy. . .hating even the
clothing stained by corrupted flesh.

JUDE 1:23 NIV

"Love the sinner, hate the sin." This is one of those clichés that doesn't appear in the Bible but is grounded in biblical truth. The Bible teaches that God hates sin and that you likewise are to hate it. Psalm 97:10 (NIV) tells you, "Let those who love the LORD hate evil."

On the other hand, the Bible enjoins believers to "love your neighbor as yourself" (Mark 12:31 NIV) and to treat others with respect. Furthermore, just as it wouldn't be loving for a doctor to refuse to tell a patient he's sick and will die unless he receives treatment, it's not loving for Christians to neglect to tell sinners that they need to be saved from eternal death.

So hate sin. Hate it so much that you will go to whatever lengths are necessary to see that people are saved from its consequences. At the same time, love the sinner so much that you'll pray for him and witness to him for as long as it takes.

God, teach me to hate evil but to love those oppressed by it.
May I show compassion to them, even though
I'm grieved by the things they do.

WORK IS A GIFT

Instead, use your hands for good hard work,
and then give generously to others in need.
EPHESIANS 4:28 NLT

◉ ◉ ◉

Work is God's idea. You may be anxious for the weekend, but God's work idea has a purpose.

While God could speak the world into existence, man needed to use his hands and skills to keep things in good shape. God made mankind so that they must use their minds to complete a job.

When you work, you can use some of the money you earn to help those who can't work. Work provides finances for meeting the needs of your family, offers a sense of purpose, initiates ideas that help others, and gives a sense of satisfaction at the end of your day.

If you think of work as a drudgery to endure, you miss the point. Work of any kind gives you a means of helping others with something God has given you.

Your perspective of your work will change when you view it as a gift that has the ability to bless others, honor God, and keep your mind focused.

I thank You for my work, dear God! Thank You for the parts
I really enjoy, and thank You for the less enjoyable parts
that You give me the grace and strength to accomplish.

TALKING TO YOURSELF

Why, my soul, are you downcast? Why so disturbed
within me? Put your hope in God, for I will yet praise
him, my Savior and my God.

PSALM 42:5 NIV

Do you ever look at the difficulties and trials in your life and then start talking to yourself? At some point or another, you may have thought:

There's no way out of this.

Things aren't going to get better. . .at least not anytime soon.

This is just the way things are going to be for me—there's nothing I can do about it.

This just isn't fair!

You know to be careful not to listen to the voices of the world and of the devil. But it's also important that you don't allow your own voice to drown out your heavenly Father. When you find yourself muttering about the hopelessness of your situation, turn your attention to the Lord, who is big enough to take control of everything going on around you.

As the apostle Peter said, "Cast all your anxiety on him because he cares for you" (1 Peter 5:7 NIV).

Dear Lord, forgive me for dwelling on my difficulties and thinking
negative thoughts. Help me to trust that You will turn these
situations around. Help me not to lose hope!

ELIJAH, MENTOR TO ELISHA

Elijah and Elisha were on their way from Gilgal.

2 KINGS 2:1 NIV

Elisha's relationship to his mentor, Elijah, was essential to his growth. Elisha couldn't have fulfilled God's call on his life without Elijah. From the scripture about the last day they were together, you discover five essential qualities of a mentor (2 Kings 2:1–18).

First, Elijah and Elisha were close. Elisha knew that the time had come for them to part, but he put off the final goodbye as long as he could. Elisha kept refusing to leave Elijah.

Second, Elijah was selfless, willing to give of himself to Elisha even at the last moment. "Tell me, what can I do for you before I am taken from you?" (2 Kings 2:9 NIV).

Third, Elijah continued to teach his mentee, demonstrating practices that Elisha needed to complete his journey (2 Kings 2:8, 14).

Fourth, Elijah invested in Elisha. He spent time with Elisha and taught him after Elisha obeyed the call to follow him (1 Kings 19:19–21).

Fifth, Elijah had what Elisha wanted—the mantle, which represented the power and presence of God. Mentors can be a big help to us.

God, help me to have a close relationship with other godly men, just like Elisha had with Elijah. Help me to follow their examples.

LOVE DOES NO HARM

Love does no harm to a neighbor;
therefore love is the fulfillment of the law.
ROMANS 13:10 NKJV

The five books of Moses contained the law of God, and the overwhelming majority of these laws boiled down to this simple precept: do no harm to your neighbor. Paul said that if you loved your neighbor you'd automatically fulfill the law, because you'd avoid harming him. That's why you must allow your life to be ruled by God's love.

As a man, you may feel that you must be rough and tough; you can't let anyone push you around; you must be assertive in business dealings and never show weakness. Loving others and being gentle may seem soft and weak.

Not so. You can be gentle to the weak yet still be tough when you need to be. You can be assertive in business dealings; adding love to the mix simply makes you honest and fair. You can act justly toward others without letting anyone push you around. Loving others takes courage and strength and proves you're a true man of God.

Dear Lord, help me to do no harm to my fellow man
in my personal life and in my business dealings.
Help me to be strong, but also ruled by Your love.

SPEAKING OF OTHERS

A gossip betrays a confidence,
but a trustworthy person keeps a secret.

PROVERBS 11:13 NIV

You may have a pretty good handle on avoiding the "biggies" where sin is concerned. You don't commit murder or adultery, and you'd never think of stealing.

But you may not be so careful when it comes to how you talk about other people. Without giving it much thought, you may make less-than-edifying comments about family members, people you work with, your spiritual leaders. . .the list goes on and on.

The Bible has plenty to say about someone who speaks ill of other people, and none of it is good. Take a look at these descriptive biblical (KJV) words for someone who engages in gossip: backbiter (Psalm 15:3), busybody (1 Timothy 5:13), inventor of evil things (Romans 1:30), talebearer (Proverbs 11:13), and whisperer (Proverbs 16:28).

God takes the things you say about others seriously, and tells you in His Word that gossip (even when what you say is factually true) carries very serious consequences—here in this world and in the world to come.

God, I pray that You would fill my heart with love and concern
for others, so that when I open my mouth to speak about
them, I speak only good and encouraging things.

EXCELLING AT WORK

Do you see a man who excels in his work? He will stand before kings; he will not stand before unknown men.

PROVERBS 22:29 NKJV

It's easy to get caught up in working only for wages, but Christians are called to work for the glory of God (Colossians 3:17). A man who excels in his work is diligent. He studies what's in place and tweaks it to make it better. He knows the needs of his customers and exceeds them. He is prompt, accurate, and quick to make adjustments when he sees the need.

Joseph was sold into slavery, but worked hard and found favor with Pharaoh, who elevated Joseph to second-in-command. He literally stood before royalty, as the above verse says. But even those of us who never meet nobility will stand before the King of kings someday.

What would it look like for you to excel? Would it mean loving an unlovable boss? Would it mean allowing him to take credit for your ideas? Would it mean going above and beyond your work description to benefit the company?

Lord, help me to excel in my work, to do my best, to cause people to think about You, the God who inspires me to do good work.

TRANSFORMERS

And we all. . .are being transformed into his image.

2 CORINTHIANS 3:18 NIV

⬡ ⬡ ⬡

Paul outlined the process of transformation in 2 Corinthians 3:18.

First, believers encounter God with *"unveiled faces."* All pretense and self-righteousness are stripped away. You see yourself clearly and know who and what you are—a sinner in need of a Savior, a weakling in need of strength, and a fool in need of wisdom.

Second, you *"contemplate the Lord's glory."* Like Moses, you're transformed by pressing into the glory of God. You grasp His true majesty and the infinite wonder of His love. You're overwhelmed in His presence.

Third, all this *"comes from the Lord."* You can't do any of it! No matter how hard you try, how disciplined, rule-keeping, or religious you are, you remain a sinner. If God doesn't change you, you can't change.

Fourth, you're *"transformed into his image."* Your destiny is to be like Jesus!

Finally, you're transformed *"with ever-increasing glory."* Transformation is a process, not an event. You keep changing and will never experience all the glory He longs to give you.

Dear God, please continue to work in my life day after day,
even on days when I feel far from You, unspiritual,
and unworthy. Thank You that You never give up on me.

LOVE GIVES. . .IT HAS TO

*"Do not be afraid, little flock, for your Father
has been pleased to give you the kingdom."*

LUKE 12:32 NIV

The apostle John wrote that "God is love" (1 John 4:8 NIV), and Jesus Himself said that God loved sinful and fallen humankind so much that He gave His most precious gift: His one and only Son (John 3:16).

That's just the nature of love, isn't it? Love, by its very nature, has no choice but to give. Real love can't just be hidden away in the heart; it must find expression through gifts to its object. And the God who identifies Himself as the perfect embodiment of love doesn't just give. . .He gives *joyfully* and He gives *perfectly*.

This perfect, giving love is what the apostle James was pointing to when he wrote, "Every good and perfect gift is from above, coming down from the Father of the heavenly lights, who does not change like shifting shadows" (James 1:17 NIV).

Your God is perfect—perfect in His holiness and perfect in His giving love. He always has been, and He always will be.

*Heavenly Father, thank You for Your love and the gifts You
give me by Your Spirit. I'm grateful that You knew
exactly what You were doing when You made me.*

ALL EYES ARE UPON YOU

*"Let your light so shine before men, that they may see your
good works and glorify your Father in heaven."*

MATTHEW 5:16 NKJV

People are watching you and constantly judging whether you live
what you preach. This includes other Christians and your children.
That's why Paul said, "Be an example to all believers in what you
say, in the way you live" (1 Timothy 4:12 NLT).

Unbelievers are watching, too—including those who are looking
for an excuse to criticize. Peter says, "It is God's will that your
honorable lives should silence those ignorant people" (1 Peter
2:15 NLT).

People are constantly watching you. It's God's *plan*—one of
His chief ways of letting the world see what the Gospel can do for
a person. Jesus said that believers are a city set on a hilltop where
everyone can see them and think about them.

People are *especially* watching when you go through hardships.
Paul said, "God has displayed us. . .we have been made a spectacle
to the world" (1 Corinthians 4:9 NKJV). How you act when you're
suffering communicates more effectively than a sermon.

*Dear God, help me to live for the truth wholeheartedly,
knowing that people are watching to see if my
faith is genuine. In Jesus' name, I ask. Amen.*

EMPTY JARS

Yet you, LORD, are our Father. We are the clay,
you are the potter; we are all the work of your hand.

ISAIAH 64:8 NIV

It's a natural thing to think that *you* are the reason you exist. It's the story of human history once mankind "did not think it worthwhile to retain the knowledge of God" (Romans 1:28 NIV). It's an ignorance that has become part of humanity's DNA.

Man was designed to be filled. A potter makes vessels empty for a purpose. That design feature is what drives man. But it's a vain pursuit without God, as King Solomon—who tested everything to fill his void—declared: "Meaningless! Meaningless! . . . Everything is meaningless!" (Ecclesiastes 12:8 NIV).

The flesh and the world promise to fill the emptiness inside, but they will always leave you empty. Even good things, apart from God, leave you unfulfilled. At best, the life of a good, successful, decent man is a life of distractions, if done without purpose. Only in God—God, your Potter—will you find the purpose you were designed for.

Father, You designed me down to the tiniest details in my DNA
helix. You drew up the living blueprint for my body and mind,
and formed me. I am in awe of You, O God!

GOD'S CAUTION TAPE

*Fix your attention on God. You'll be changed from the
inside out. Readily recognize what he wants
from you, and quickly respond to it.*

ROMANS 12:2 MSG

What if there was the equivalent of yellow caution tape when it
came to places, circumstances, and events that you should avoid?
You'd surely pay attention!

If you go to the theater and the movie doesn't look like it
matches God's heart, imagine yellow caution tape warning you to
keep out. Imagine the same for individuals the Bible describes as
"bad company." Or maybe you need to avoid arguments.

God's Holy Spirit came to be that "caution tape." You don't
see visible warning signs, but if you pay attention, you'll recognize
those warnings as clearly as seeing bright yellow tape blocking
the way to a dangerous area.

God has always provided the warning signs—you just need to
recognize them. God gave you the help you need—you just need to
stop rejecting it. If you humble yourself and fix your attention on
God and the guidance He provides in His Spirit, He will help you.

*Lord, help me to pay close attention when You whisper to my
heart that I shouldn't go somewhere, shouldn't watch a certain
show, or shouldn't say those words that enter my mind.*

SETTING AN EXAMPLE

Join together in following my example.
PHILIPPIANS 3:17 NIV

Every man who seeks God is leading the way for others. The question is, are you living up to the life of Christ in you, or are you slipping back into old habits and patterns?

Paul knew his life was being watched. His example mattered. Your children, your friends, and the unbelievers who surround you every day are watching, too. You may not think about it, but it's true. Paul took that responsibility seriously.

To be a good example, you ought to follow the example of others who are ahead of you on the path of spiritual growth. Paul wrote, "Keep your eyes on those who live as we do" (Philippians 3:17 NIV). You set an example by following the example of others.

Moreover, you must have integrity. It isn't about putting your best foot forward or presenting a handsome veneer that hides the truth. How you handle your flaws and failures, how you deal with challenges and difficulties, and how you respond to temptation are part of that example.

Men of true integrity are in short supply. Determine to be one.

*Dear Lord, help me to aspire to be like the godly men
I admire. And help my example, weak and imperfect
as it is, to inspire others to live for You.*

SAY SOMETHING

Everyone enjoys a fitting reply; it is wonderful
to say the right thing at the right time!
PROVERBS 15:23 NLT

◉ ◉ ◉

Some people always know the right thing to say. And they often know what to say to encourage others when they're down. But what if you're not a mind reader, especially when it comes to people's emotions? And what if you're not that communicative? What if, like so many men, you're the strong, silent type?

Solomon wrote, "The heartfelt counsel of a friend is as sweet as perfume" (Proverbs 27:9 NLT), and he was talking to men, too. Note that this counsel is effective because it's "heartfelt." As long as what you say is caring, it doesn't matter if it lacks eloquence. The most important thing is that the person knows you *care* for him or her.

Even if you're quiet, you can still say something, no matter how awkwardly you express yourself. So what if you can't read a person's emotions? You can find out where they're at by gently asking. You can say the right thing at the right time even if you stumble all over yourself saying it.

Father, please give me the words to say to those who desperately
need to know that I care. Give me the courage to
speak with genuine love and concern.

HARDWIRED FOR SUCCESS

*Earn a reputation for living well in God's eyes
and the eyes of the people.*

PROVERBS 3:4 MSG

Men seem to be hardwired to want to be considered a success. Go to most ten-year high school reunions and men will talk about how successful they are, or they may resort to reliving their high school successes.

Men will do what they feel they have to in order to shore up the appearance of success. However, when failure comes, some men will shift directions completely. These men will embrace failure as an old friend and live as if success is no longer available.

God longs for men to be fighters for what's right. He longs for you to stop believing that if you just try hard enough you can move everything in your favor.

Your greatest success is to be a *forgiven* man of God, to be in right relationship with Him. So focus your efforts on knowing and pleasing Him. Then, as you put your attention on what your heavenly Father thinks, what others think won't matter so much.

*God, help me to be concerned about what You think
and to try to please You. Then I know I'll be truly successful,
no matter what my life looks like to others.*

HONORING DISCIPLINE AND COMMITMENT

Join with me in suffering, like a good soldier of Christ Jesus.
No one serving as a soldier gets entangled in civilian affairs,
but rather tries to please his commanding officer.

2 TIMOTHY 2:3–4 NIV

Paul looked to soldiers as an ideal of single-minded commitment and devotion to a cause. According to Paul, the model soldier prioritizes the wishes of a commanding officer and avoids the distractions of civilians. A good soldier exists for the single purpose of carrying out the orders of his commanding officer. Soldiers won't leave their ranks to argue with civilians or even to address their own affairs. Their primary concern is their mission.

The "soldiers" of Christ win by losing, patiently enduring suffering, and responding to the surrounding culture with humility and meekness. There are many "civilian affairs" that can pull you away from the purposes of God, from entertainment to accumulating wealth to arguing. You'll carry out your Commanding Officer's mission most effectively when you learn from the disciplined focus of soldiers who carry out their orders under even the most demanding circumstances.

Dear God, help me to be a good soldier. Help me to stand strong despite suffering for Your sake. Don't let me become distracted by the cares of this world. In Jesus' name, I pray. Amen.

VARIABLE RATE DEBT

*"In prayer there is a connection between what God does and
what you do. You can't get forgiveness from God, for instance,
without also forgiving others. If you refuse to do your
part, you cut yourself off from God's part."*
MATTHEW 6:14-15 MSG

If you have a variable rate loan, then you know that your rate could
go up or down. Forgiveness works in a similar way. When others
hurt you, it can be easy to think of it like a loan. By offending you,
they have taken on a debt that you want repaid.

While you keep track of what the offender owes, he may be
unaware that a debt is owed. No matter how much interest you
tack on to someone's debt, many offenders will never meet your
repayment expectations.

Offenses happen. When you refuse to forgive, you don't gain
anything—you cut yourself off from God, who expects you to extend
the same forgiveness He has given you. When you're quick to
forgive, you'll discover that you save a lot of time and emotional
energy. . .and you stay connected to God.

---

*God, please help me to be quick to forgive. Please free me from
carrying grudges for months or even years. Help me to keep
a clean ledger and forgive as I want to be forgiven.*

RETREAT AFTER SUCCESS

Yet the news about him spread all the more, so that crowds
of people came to hear him and to be healed of their
sicknesses. But Jesus often withdrew to
lonely places and prayed.
LUKE 5:15–16 NIV

Whenever you experience success, you naturally think of ways to keep it going and build on it. Jesus had the opposite response. As the crowds seeking Him increased, He withdrew to be with God, to maintain His connection with the Father. When Jesus experienced success or His schedule started to fill up, He recognized that was the time to pause.

Building on success isn't necessarily the best thing for your soul. Instead, you should take measured steps away from your work in pursuit of spiritual renewal. This doesn't mean leaving your work behind and setting off for a lengthy wilderness retreat.

Whenever you have a free moment, your first move should be toward prayer, reflection on scripture, or just reflection on your day so that you know how to pray. You can find time to pray even for a few minutes. Then you'll always find the time to get your work done.

God, please help me to discipline myself to take quiet time with
You, and not just in the morning, but throughout the
day—especially when I experience success.

BETTER DAYS AHEAD

"You will surely forget your trouble,
recalling it only as waters gone by."
JOB 11:16 NIV

Sometimes you're made to pass through a valley of suffering, and you may not even be certain that you'll survive. It looks like you'll crash. Perhaps you disobeyed God, or you acted rashly or inconsiderately to others, and now the consequences of your actions are rising like floodwaters. Or perhaps problems have come upon you for no fault of your own.

Yet, difficult as your circumstances may be, soon enough you'll be laughing again and will forget your troubles. They'll be as waters that have evaporated. David said of God, "For his anger lasts only a moment, but his favor lasts a lifetime; weeping may stay for the night, but rejoicing comes in the morning" (Psalm 30:5 NIV).

God doesn't get any pleasure out of causing His children to suffer. He does allow suffering, true, but it usually only lasts long enough to bring about good in your life. "The LORD comforts his people and will have compassion on his afflicted ones" (Isaiah 49:13 NIV).

Dear Father, I trust You that this time of suffering will eventually
pass. Thank You that You will once again give me joy.
I thank You for all that You do in my life.

IF YOU MISSED THE BLESSING

"God bless you and keep you, God smile on you and gift you,
God look you full in the face and make you prosper."
NUMBERS 6:24-26 MSG

What you believed about yourself when you were a child is likely what you believe today. In many ways, you may believe what you were told by your parents, friends, or bullies. You still carry invisible tattoos reading *last to be picked*, *slow*, *stupid*, or *worthless*.

On bad days, you'll believe what someone said when you were five. It doesn't matter if it's true or not; you'll accept it as true even when the evidence suggests otherwise.

If no one has ever spoken a blessing into your life, consider this: before you were born, God knew your name, fit you together in your mother's womb, and called you a masterpiece (Psalm 139:13–16). He created you for something only you can do.

You'll sin, but God can forgive you. He will never abandon you. He has always loved you, and He still has a plan for you.

Don't pay attention to what others call you; pay attention to His call.

God, whatever I may think on my worst days, whatever others
may think about me, You loved me before I was even born,
and You blessed me. Help me to always remember that.

THE NATURE OF LOVE

*If I have a faith that can move mountains, but do not have
love, I am nothing. If I give all I possess to the poor...
that I may boast, but do not have love, I gain nothing.*

1 CORINTHIANS 13:2–3 NIV

You may wonder, "How could I give all that I possess to alleviate
the suffering of the poor, and *not* have love? Isn't such giving a clear
proof of love?" But Paul clarifies that if you have selfish motives
for doing so, you'll gain nothing.

Paul goes on in verses 4–7 to give the definition of love. Love
is *not* boastful or easily angered; love is patient, kind, humble; it
honors others, seeks others' benefit, and keeps no record of wrongs.
So it's not enough to go through an outward show of charity.

Jesus promised that if you have great faith you can say to a
mountain, "Be removed and be cast into the sea" (Matthew 21:21
NKJV), but Paul added, "If I have a faith that can move mountains,
but do not have love, I am nothing." So love God and others.

---

*Lord, help me to truly love, to be motivated by love in all that I do,
not merely go through the motions of being generous and caring.*

GOD PROTECTS YOU

The Lord is faithful, and he will strengthen you
and protect you from the evil one.

2 THESSALONIANS 3:3 NIV

God can strengthen you so you can resist the onslaughts of the devil. These may be negative thoughts, sexual temptation, waves of fear, accidents, inexplicable illnesses, or many other things. Fortunately, you don't need to depend on your *own* strength to withstand them.

Jesus instructed believers to pray, "Our Father in heaven.... deliver us from the evil one" (Matthew 6:9, 13 NIV). Since Jesus commanded you to pray this, you can certainly expect that God will answer. Jesus told His Father, "My prayer is...that you protect them from the evil one" (John 17:15 NIV). Jesus is also praying for the Father to protect you.

Paul stated, "The Lord is *faithful*, and he *will* strengthen you and protect you from the evil one" (2 Thessalonians 3:3 NIV, emphasis added). Of course, you need to put forth some effort. As Ephesians 6 says, you must stand your ground, hold on to your shield of faith, and resist the devil. If you remain steadfast, God will make you victorious.

Dear Father, please hear my prayer. I'm under spiritual
attack. I need Your help today! Please deliver me
from the evil one. In Jesus' name, I pray. Amen.

JESUS CHRIST, CREATOR AND SUSTAINER

In these last days [God] has spoken to us by his Son...through whom also he made the universe. The Son is the radiance of God's glory and the exact representation of his being, sustaining all things by his powerful word.

HEBREWS 1:2–3 NIV

We can never honor Jesus Christ too much. Let's consider two ways He is honored in relation to all things.

1. **As the Creator of the universe.** The fact that Jesus is the Creator of all things is taught in John 1:3, Colossians 1:16, and other scriptures. *You* are part of His creation. Sometimes you have a hard time feeling a sense of self-worth. This isn't something you strive to obtain. Instead, it's something God has breathed into you from the very beginning.

2. **As the Sustainer of the universe.** You are sustained, not by your own strength, but by Jesus Christ. You experience that strengthening as you read the Bible, meditate on it, pray, worship Him, read devotions, spend time with other Christians, love your neighbors, and share your faith with them.

Lord Jesus, I praise You as the Creator of all universes— the physical realms I can see and the endless invisible realms. I praise You for sustaining it all...even my own life.

JESUS CHRIST, SAVIOR AND LORD

After he [Jesus Christ] had provided purification for sins,
he sat down at the right hand of the Majesty in heaven.

HEBREWS 1:3 NIV

Let's consider the third and fourth ways that Jesus Christ is honored in relation to all things.

3. As the Savior of the universe. Romans 8:20–21, Colossians 1:19–20, and other scriptures tell you that Jesus intends to redeem creation itself. But, very importantly, He "provided purification for [your] sins."

4. As the Lord of the universe. The phrase "he sat down" spoke powerfully to the first readers, because they knew that priests never sat down. Jesus could sit because His work was complete. He is now supremely honored in heaven. What's more, in His position of authority, Christ intercedes with the Father on your behalf.

The writer of Hebrews continually exalts the Son of God, since he is convinced that the power and majesty of Jesus Christ's person are the answer to all questions on earth. Does your life sometimes feel stressful and even overwhelming? If so, the answer to your problems is *who Jesus Christ is. . .in you.*

Dear Jesus, I worship You because You're the only Savior,
the only way to Your Father. And I worship You
because You are supreme Lord over all.

MEDITATE ON GOD

Be still, and know that I am God.
PSALM 46:10 KJV

There's a time to earnestly pray for what you need. But there is *also* a time to meditate, to think deeply on who God is. At times like that, focus entirely on Him and keep your mind from wandering. God will reward you with a deeper knowledge of His nature and love.

God commanded, "Be still, and know that I am God" (Psalm 46:10 KJV). You are to still your heart and focus on knowing Him—that He is almighty God, supreme, holy, beautiful, and glorious.

You should also meditate on the wonderful things God has done in your life and in the lives of others. Think of His miracles, both great and small. "I meditate on all Your works; I muse on the work of Your hands" (Psalm 143:5 NKJV).

When you read the Bible, pause at a verse and meditate deeply on its meaning. "Oh, how I love Your law! It is my meditation all the day" (Psalm 119:97 NKJV). Meditate on God and the things of God today.

Dear Father in heaven, may I meditate on You and Your Word, not only now, but throughout the day. Please give me deep spiritual insight into who You are. In Jesus' name, I ask.

OVERTHINKING AND UNDER-PRAYING

Do not be anxious about anything, but in every situation,
by prayer and petition, with thanksgiving,
present your requests to God.

PHILIPPIANS 4:6 NIV

The Bible speaks about some very intelligent men. Joseph is described as discerning and wise (Genesis 41:39); of Daniel and his companions it's recorded that "God gave [them] knowledge and understanding" (Daniel 1:17 NIV); to Solomon was granted "wisdom and very great insight" (1 Kings 4:29 NIV).

In their days, these men were renowned for their intellect, and God used all of them to accomplish His will. But their real strength came from knowing the source of their gifts and the necessity of meeting God in prayer.

Prayer doesn't replace knowledge, wisdom, or discernment—it transcends it. Prayer is inviting the God of all wisdom to participate in your life. He delights in trading His peace for your anxiety. Thinking won't get you out of every situation, but He "is able to do immeasurably more than all we ask or imagine" (Ephesians 3:20 NIV).

Always ask God for wisdom (James 1:5), remembering that the greatest wisdom of all is to come to God in prayer.

Lord, I ask You to give me the wisdom I need. I can't resolve
my problems on my own. I need a supernatural
solution. Help me, please!

GLOWING IN THE DARK

When. . .all the Israelites saw Moses, his face was radiant.

EXODUS 34:30 NIV

It's one of the Bible's most powerful moments. Moses returned from the presence of the Lord glowing (Exodus 34:29–35)! In 2 Corinthians 3:7–18 (NIV), Paul used this moment to illustrate the transformation believers experience in the presence of God. "And we all, who with unveiled faces contemplate the Lord's glory, are being transformed into his image with ever-increasing glory" (verse 18).

Tremendous spiritual transformation isn't just possible—it's real! God does a powerful work in you to transform you into Christ's image. That is your great and glorious hope!

Great spiritual transformation should be observable. Those around you should notice the difference not because of pious posturing but because you're truly different. It isn't something you put on display. It's something you can't hide!

Finally, great spiritual vitality can only be renewed in the presence of God. When the glory faded, Moses took off the veil and returned to the source of true transformation (Exodus 34:33–35). When he needed more of God, God was there for him. He's there for you, too.

God, help me to seek Your face and be continually refilled with Your Spirit, to be so united with You that I'm transformed into Your image.

FEELING LIKE A FAILURE

God is not unjust; he will not forget your work and the love
you have shown him as you have helped his people.
HEBREWS 6:10 NIV

Sometimes you may feel like a failure, as if your whole life of attempting to serve God has amounted to nothing. Isaiah once felt frustration, too. "I said, 'I have labored in vain; I have spent my strength for nothing at all. Yet what is due me is in the LORD's hand, and my reward is with my God' " (Isaiah 49:4 NIV). Even though he was despondent, he still couldn't help but believe that God would reward him.

Hebrews 6:10 (NIV) says, "God is not unjust; he will not forget your work and the love you have shown him as you have helped his people." He sees everything you do and will surely reward you. "Whoever is kind to the poor lends to the LORD, and he will reward them for what they have done" (Proverbs 19:17 NIV).

It's worth it to serve the Lord. You may feel like you've failed, but God sees your faithfulness.

Lord, even though I feel like a failure at times, I know
You will reward me. Help me not to beat myself up.
Help me to see Your hand and Your mercy in my life.

AFTER...

*After you have suffered a little while, [God] will himself
restore you and make you strong, firm and steadfast.*

1 PETER 5:10 NIV

Peter reminds you that when you're tested you suffer for "a little while" (1 Peter 4:10 NIV). It doesn't feel that way. Pain stretches time.

But you need to understand "a little while" not in terms of this life but in terms of eternity. This life is a quickly evaporating vapor. For those who overcome, joy everlasting awaits. You are "called... to his eternal glory in Christ" (verse 10).

Tests purify you, temper you, and make you stronger. Testing won't destroy you. It prepares you for the next great step in your spiritual journey.

Perhaps the most comforting words in this passage are found in 1 Peter 5:11 (NIV): "To him be the power for ever and ever. Amen." There has never been and will never be a time when God is not sovereign.

In times of testing, life feels out of control. It *may* be out of your control. But it isn't out of the control of the God who loved you from before time and who has dominion over all things.

*God, thank You for keeping me through fiery tests.
I know Your will is being done, even when it
seems like things are out of control.*

KEEP YOUR WORD

Above all, my brothers and sisters, do not swear—not by heaven or by earth or by anything else. All you need to say is a simple "Yes" or "No." Otherwise you will be condemned.

JAMES 5:12 NIV

Have you ever known someone you knew you could depend on? The kind of guy who you knew would keep his word when he told you he would help you with an unpleasant task like moving or painting your house?

That's the kind of friend we'd all like to have, isn't it? But it's also the kind of friend you should strive to be.

Some Christians take the words of the above Bible verse literally, avoiding making any kind of promises, taking any kind of oaths, or entering into contracts. But even for someone who doesn't follow this verse by the letter, James' words strongly imply a simple but important principle: *be a man who can be taken at his word.*

Be a man who is so dependable that no one ever has to ask, "Do you promise?" Be a man whose "yes" always means "yes" and whose "no" always means "no."

Lord, help me to be a man of my word, one who remembers appointments, keeps promises, and shows up on time. Give me a conviction of how important this is, I pray.

LISTENING IS A DANGEROUS ACTIVITY

Herod feared John and protected him, knowing him to be
a righteous and holy man. When Herod heard John,
he was greatly puzzled; yet he liked to listen to him.

MARK 6:20 NIV

John the Baptist was the first prophet to come along after what has been called the "Four Hundred Silent Years" in Israel's history. During the time between the last prophet of the Old Testament and John, no prophets spoke to the people.

So when John the Baptist showed up, looking and acting like the greatest prophet in Israel's history (Mark 1:6), people flocked to him. Even tax collectors and soldiers came to ask his advice (Luke 3:12–14). John didn't hold back his message even with Herod the tetrarch, publicly rebuking him for adultery. That landed John in prison and ultimately cost him his life (Matthew 14:6–12).

Herod made the worst mistake a person can when it comes to the Good News—he treated it like entertainment. He listened without changing. Listening is dangerous business if you don't intend to apply what you hear from God.

Father in heaven, may I hear and obey Your Word—not only
listen and mentally assent to it, but put it into practice.
Convict me in areas where I haven't been obedient, I pray.

DON'T LOSE FAITH

The children of Ephraim, being armed and carrying bows,
turned back in the day of battle.

PSALM 78:9 NKJV

The men of Israel had been called to battle, so they assembled their armies and marched forth, armed with swords and shields and carrying bows and arrows. But when the tribe of Ephraim saw the enemy, they turned back. Although they had trained for war and were well armed, they lost their nerve. They didn't believe that God was with them.

This applies to challenges you face as well. You could be fully trained in your profession and have all the tools you need, but if a situation seems overwhelming, you may throw up your hands before you even start.

One time Moses doubted that he could do what God had commanded him, so the Lord asked, "What is that in your hand?" Moses answered, "A rod" (Exodus 4:2 NKJV). It didn't seem like much, but God proceeded to do astounding miracles when Moses held it up.

Never underestimate your ability to do what God asks you to do. When He is with you, you can do amazing things.

Dear God, help me not to give up in despair before I even
begin. Give me vision and courage to face the battles
I must fight, knowing that You will help me.

TAKE HOLD OF HIM

I press on to take hold of that for which
Christ Jesus took hold of me.
PHILIPPIANS 3:12 NIV

Sometimes the prize seems elusive, just out of reach. You shouldn't be surprised. The more you grow in Christ, the more you realize how little you truly know Him. In Philippians 3:12–14, Paul outlined his strategy for taking hold of more and more of God in his life.

First, don't expect to ever truly reach that goal. Paul didn't.

Second, the more Christ takes hold of you, the more you're captivated by His power and presence in your life, and the more you're motivated to pursue Him.

Third, forget. Let the past, with its mistakes and failures, stay in the past. Don't long for what you had yesterday. Backward focus prevents forward motion.

Fourth, press on. The word translated "press on" means "to run swiftly in order to catch a person or thing." Just as athletes approaching the finish line lean into the tape, you should exert every effort and lean into God.

Finally, there's a prize! It's so wonderful that it's more than enough to keep you in the race!

Father, give me the determination to take firm hold of the promise of eternal life in Jesus. Help me never to lose the heavenly vision.

THE JOY OF SUFFERING

*Dear friends, do not be surprised at the fiery ordeal that has
come on you to test you, as though something strange were
happening to you. But rejoice inasmuch as you participate
in the sufferings of Christ, so that you may be
overjoyed when his glory is revealed.*

1 PETER 4:12–13 NIV

Suffering and opposition for the sake of Christ isn't just a sign
that you have cast your lot with Jesus. Suffering is a way to meet
with Christ on a deeper level. As you face opposition, slander, or
worse, you create a space in your life to more fully experience
Christ. By choosing to suffer for Him, you're denying your own
desires and sinful nature.

Most importantly, by choosing to suffer, you're taking a step
to believe that God has something better for you. You have the
hope of His glory one day. While your desires promise you joy and
fulfillment in the short term, these are fleeting and can't compare
to the joy you can experience today in the presence of the Lord—let
alone when you're united with Him one day.

*Dear Lord, help me to gladly accept suffering for Your name.
Use it to draw me closer to You. Help me to
experience Your presence, I pray.*

FORETASTES OF HEAVEN

*"The blind receive sight, the lame walk, those who have
leprosy are cleansed, the deaf hear, the dead are raised,
and the good news is proclaimed to the poor."*

LUKE 7:22 NIV

Jesus Christ's earthly ministry gave people a foretaste of what
His eternal kingdom is like. They saw individuals raised from the
dead, others healed spiritually, others healed physically, and still
others healed psychologically.

As a follower of Jesus Christ, you know your sins past, present,
and future are already forgiven, yet you experience His forgiveness
anew each time you confess your sins. Immediately afterward, you
want to pause and savor the experience of being forgiven. If you
do, you enjoy a delicious foretaste of heaven.

Even though your salvation is all-encompassing, it doesn't
mean you don't sin—any more than it means you never get sick,
never suffer trials, never wrestle with temptation, never fail, never
fear cancer, and never end up dying. Aren't these the means of
helping you to continue longing for heaven?

Slow down and savor each foretaste experience this side of
eternity. These are Jesus Christ's rich and valuable gifts to you.

---

*Dear Jesus, as I spend time in Your presence, I get a taste of
what heaven will be like. Help me to count all the ways
You give me a foreshadowing of the riches of Your kingdom.*

RECOVERING THE LOST

If you know people who have wandered off from God's truth,
don't write them off. Go after them. Get them back and you
will have rescued precious lives from destruction.

JAMES 5:20 MSG

It's easy to write off people who have drifted from the faith. You tell yourself that they knew full well what they were doing when they went back to their worldly ways. But the question is, are you *concerned* about them? Do you pray for them and reach out to them? Jesus said:

> *"What man of you, having a hundred sheep,*
> *if he loses one of them, does not leave the*
> *ninety-nine in the wilderness, and go after the*
> *one which is lost until he finds it?"*
> (Luke 15:4 NKJV)

Jesus took it for granted that *every* person listening would be motivated to scour the desert for a lost sheep, asking, "What man does *not* go after it until he finds it?" And how much more valuable is a person than a sheep?

In the end, the person must make up his own mind to return to the Lord, but you can be a big part of helping restore him.

Lord, I know people—even family members—who have drifted
from You. Please use my example, my words,
and my concern to draw them back to You.

THE VALUE OF BETRAYAL

"Because the patriarchs were jealous of Joseph, they sold him as a slave into Egypt. But God... gave Joseph wisdom and enabled him to gain the goodwill of Pharaoh king of Egypt. So Pharaoh made him ruler over Egypt and all his palace."

ACTS 7:9-10 NIV

Betrayal isn't usually part of the recommended route to success. But in Joseph's case it was essential. His brothers hated him, so they sold him into slavery. Because of this, Joseph ended up in charge of all Egypt and was able to rescue his family from famine.

Betrayal was part of God's plan for Joseph. The hardest experiences in your life can be tools for God's use. Disappointment can clarify your expectations by stripping away false hopes. Tragedy can work its painful service to show you the reality of a world that isn't your home.

Joseph remained faithful to God during his afflictions until God's timing was complete and he became the savior of all Israel. In this, Joseph was a foreshadowing of Jesus, who also endured betrayal as part of God's will in order to save His people.

God, please give me more of an eternal perspective on my problems. Help me to know that even if others betray, curse, or mistreat me, You will bring good out of it.

FROM THE MESS, VALUE

Where no oxen are, the trough is clean;
but much increase comes by the strength of an ox.

PROVERBS 14:4 NKJV

Oxen are messy creatures. But there's no way to take advantage of their strength without having to watch where you step. If you want to produce something of value, you're going to have to deal with the mess it causes.

It's risky to run a business—people don't always do what you expect, customers demand more than you can provide, and every week you have to clean up a mess.

Marriage, for all its delights, can generate piles of debris. Sacrificing dreams, working through conflict, dealing with in-laws, negotiating finances, serving when you would prefer to be served—all these make for a mess. But the rewards are worth it.

Having kids may be literally and figuratively the messiest choice of all. But most parents would tell you they'd do it all over again.

Nothing of value comes without work, consequences, and risk. Laziness and fear are your main obstacles. God wants you to work at whatever He's put into your life, focusing on creating something of value.

Lord, grant me the patience to deal with messes,
knowing they're proof that things are happening in my life.
Help me to be thankful for what You're doing for me.

CARING FOR OTHERS

Don't look out only for your own interests,
but take an interest in others, too.

PHILIPPIANS 2:4 NLT

When the Bible says "take an interest in others," it's referring to *all* other people. This includes your wife, children, relatives, workmates, and total strangers. You naturally look out for yourself and take care of business that's important to you. But you're also your brother's keeper.

Take your children, for example. Because they're children, they're interested in things that long ago ceased to interest *you*. But since you love them, you make an effort to listen to their jokes, as well as pause to sympathize with their sorrows.

The Bible says, "Be willing to associate with people of low position" (Romans 12:16 NIV). This includes cousins whose interests seem boring to you. It includes an elderly relative who seems to be a relic of a bygone century. To associate with them, you have to let go of the idea that your time is too valuable.

Many people aren't willing to put forth the effort to care for others. But there are great rewards for doing so.

Dear God, give me the love I need to slow down my schedule
and take time to be with those who need me. Help me
not to ignore them. In Jesus' name. Amen.

BLESSING YOUR PARENTS

If you honor your father and mother, "things will go well for you."
EPHESIANS 6:3 NLT

What if you had one or more parents who just weren't there for you? What if they didn't have what it took to show what love should look like? What if they seemed uncaring and spoke words that couldn't be considered blessings?

You may be waiting for a blessing you've never received, validation that never came, an encouraging parent who only seemed the stuff of fairy tales, and you're in conflict. Giving a blessing to a parent who never blessed you sounds awkward.

Some parents were likely broken by an unspoken blessing that should have come from *their* parents. Even your parents may be waiting to be told they're loved.

As much as they may have hurt you, a rebuilt relationship may be possible when *you* give your *parents* a blessing. Your blessing can create a crack in the walls they've built around their hearts. If this is something you desire but feel hesitant to try, ask God to increase your love for your parents and to guide you in saying the right words.

Dear God, fill my heart with love and give me words of blessing to speak over my father and mother, even if our relationship has been imperfect and difficult.

LETTING IT PASS

Overlook an offense and bond a friendship;
fasten on to a slight and—good-bye, friend!
PROVERBS 17:9 MSG

● ● ●

Everyone makes mistakes and causes offense, but some men are especially prone to doing this. Or they borrow a valuable tool and lose it. . .then inform you that they can't replace it at this time. How do you respond?

Hopefully, you'll let go of minor offenses quickly. But it may be more difficult to forgive large losses, especially if this isn't the first time. But think carefully before you react. You can express your disappointment and calmly let others know how this makes you feel. And you usually should express your emotions.

But it's not wise to hold a grudge. Leviticus 19:18 (MSG) says, "Don't. . .carry a grudge against any of your people." It then goes on to say, "Love your neighbor as yourself," which is the whole reason you shouldn't nurse grudges.

God's commandments about love and forgiveness have practical applications in your everyday life and in your workplace. They may not be easy to implement, but they're guaranteed to work.

Dear Lord, help me not to hold on to hurt feelings or to nurse grudges. Help me to react the right way to losses and offenses. Give me both wisdom and love, I pray.

NO TURNING BACK

But now after you have known God, or rather are known by God, how is it that you turn again to the weak and beggarly elements, to which you desire again to be in bondage?

GALATIANS 4:9 NKJV

Most men tend to default to the familiar. The Jews in Galatia were no exception. After hearing the Gospel and responding to it, they knew God in a far more intimate way than when they were trying to keep the ceremonial law.

None of those practices had any inherent spiritual power. They were shadows of the Gospel to come. Yet Paul was writing to the Galatian church with a heavy heart, knowing that they had slipped back into their old ways. "I am afraid for you, lest I have labored for you in vain," he wrote in verse 11 (NKJV).

Today, you struggle with other empty rituals, such as performance-based Christianity. Formerly, you believed you could earn your way to heaven by good works. Even though you left that notion behind, you may return to it when you believe your performance is a reflection of spiritual strength. Reject such notions. Return to the power of Christ in you.

Father, help me always to bear in mind that I need Your grace to make it. Keep me from returning to my old ways of thinking and living.

HOME SWEET HOME?

As long as we are at home in the body we are away from the Lord.

2 CORINTHIANS 5:6 NIV

In 2 Corinthians 5:1–10, Paul was speaking about his struggle between life and death. He realized that this physical life in some ways kept him from being "at home" with the Lord.

There is no doubt about it. You are at home in this physical world. This planet is the one place in the universe where life is known to flourish. You were made for this place. More precisely, this world was created to be your home.

But this world as it now is isn't your home forever. You weren't meant to experience the suffering and sadness of a world broken by sin and disobedience. You were meant to enjoy intimacy with God without any barrier (Genesis 3).

Being "at home" also means being in a place where you feel comfortable, at rest, and at ease. You should not be at home with this world's values, lifestyles, and priorities. You should be restless in this world. If you aren't uncomfortable here, you'll never be truly at home with Christ.

Lord, help me to know that this present world isn't my final destination. Give me a heavenly outlook so that I value the place where I'll spend eternity with You.

PRACTICING HOSPITALITY

When God's people are in need, be ready to help them.
Always be eager to practice hospitality.
ROMANS 12:13 NLT

The Hebrews were urged to show kindness to strangers, to show hospitality by taking them into their homes (Job 31:32). They were expected to feed them and were responsible to protect guests under their roof. These days, such hospitality is rare. With so much crime and users eager to take advantage of people, it's considered dangerous and unadvisable.

But the Bible still says, "*Always* be *eager* to practice hospitality" (Romans 12:13 NLT, emphasis added). So let's look at other ways of showing hospitality. What about when a new family comes to your church, doesn't know anyone, and needs friends? Are you eager to practice hospitality? Do you and your wife invite them over for lunch? Do you help them get settled into your town?

What about when families in your church are struggling without basic needs—without warm clothes, food, or other necessities? Do you reach out in practical ways to help? There are many ways to be "a lover of hospitality" today (Titus 1:8 KJV).

Father, help me to be "eager to practice hospitality." Help me to welcome new people to my church, to befriend new Christians, and to find ways to help them.